Manhattan Atlas

In celebration of ⟨...⟩ VanDam

presents the first innov⟨...⟩ urban cartography

in 50 years: Here's what they say about VanDam:

"...A sophisticated resource..." **NEW YORK TIMES**

"The best innovation in map design since the globe

was fllattened onto paper!" **DIVERSION MAGAZINE**

"...For savvy travelers..." **PLAYBOY**

"Ingenious... A Magical series..." **TRAVEL & LEISURE**

Vent, applaud, criticize and respond: www.vandam.com.

Manhattan @tlas

Following the best–selling **NY@tlas**, first published in 1998, and by special request from people who use the city, here is **Manhattan@tlas** – the ultimate guide to the vertical city.

Manhattan@tlas organizes Gotham into three easily accessible parts:

Basics: neighborhoods, hospitals, schools, streets, and the like.

Top 100: Over 1,400 listings reveal the best in dining, attractions, architecture, film, hotels, performing arts, nightlife, shopping, sports, natural resources, theatre, education & more.

Maps: designed to clarify the "culture of congestion" these large-scale maps show you exactly how to get from here to there.

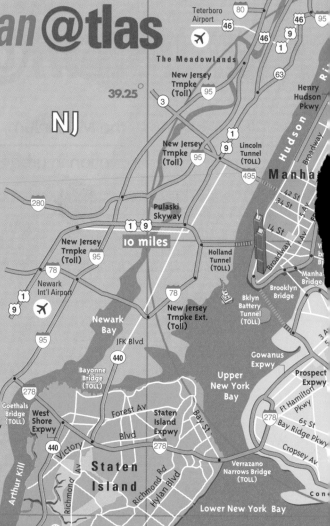

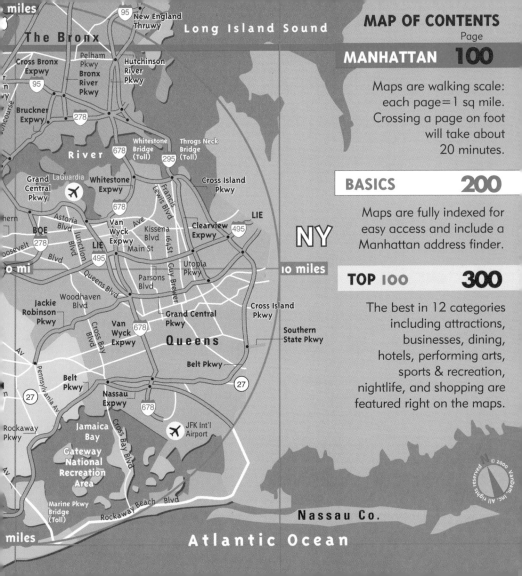

MAP OF CONTENTS

MANHATTAN **100**

Maps are walking scale: each page=1 sq mile. Crossing a page on foot will take about 20 minutes.

BASICS **200**

Maps are fully indexed for easy access and include a Manhattan address finder.

TOP 100 **300**

The best in 12 categories including attractions, businesses, dining, hotels, performing arts, sports & recreation, nightlife, and shopping are featured right on the maps.

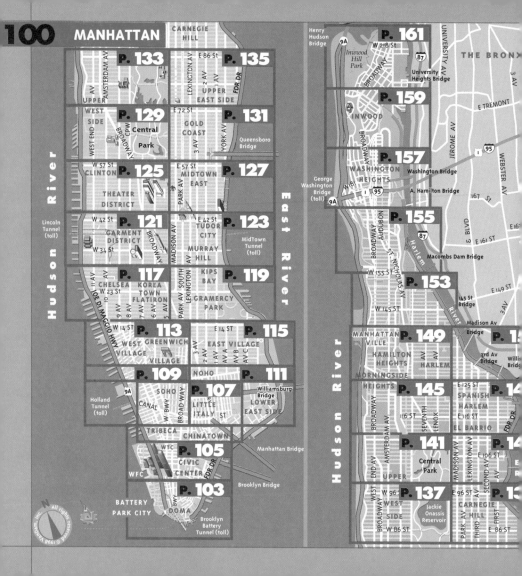

Manhattan's Best

This is the ultimate vertical city where "the Culture of Congestion" rules.

Central Park is the city's grand public square. Treasured by locals and visitors alike, it is the locus for play, pastoral love, horse—back riding, jogging, sledding, biking, rollerblading & picnics. Its Metropolitan Opera and Philharmonic concerts in the summer and the NY Marathon in November are living proof of how the uniquely American human experiment can work. **129A**

Rainbow Grill Uniquely NY! Reserve for dinner and dancing in the clouds. The "Fred & Ginger" set is an Art Deco stunner as is the prix fixe. The best views are from the Promenade Bar. 30 Rock. Plaza, 65th fl, 212-632-5100. **126A**

World Financial Center

America's most successful urban development of the 1980s opened the city to the Hudson & reinvented downtown as a destination. Sniffing the breezes on the Esplanade, one is tempted to forsake the country for the city. The free evening mambo and guajira concerts in the summer have made great strides in unwelding northerners at the hip. **104C**

The Metropolitan Museum of Art

Covering five millennia, this is the world's encyclopedia of the arts with collections too numerous to list. Favorites include the Rockefeller wing, the Egyptian galleries and the Lehman Wing. Allow for more than one visit to drink in the views of Central Park from the Roof Terrace Bar. 5 Av @ 82 St, 212-535-7710. **133B**

Lever House This classic of Corbusian modernism marked the beginning of what has become a virtual museum of modern architecture on Park Avenue. **126B**

TriBeCa Once the poor cousin of SoHo, TriBeCa (Triangle below Canal St) is now the rich Hollywood uncle. Robert de Niro's Tribeca Grill, Drew Nieporent's Montrachet and Nobu as well as Chanterelle and Danube are the temples of haute cuisine downtown. (Check top 100 Dining for details). **106C**

Chrysler Building

Despite recent plans to turn it into a hotel, William L Van Alen's classic Deco L tower remains the pièce de resistance of 1930s American skyscraper design. 405 Lexington Av, 212-682-3070. **126C**

Manhattan Stats
Population: 1.4 million
Area: 24 sq miles

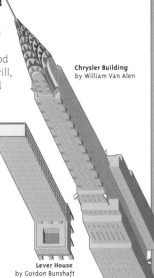

Chrysler Building
by William Van Alen

Lever House
by Gordon Bunshaft

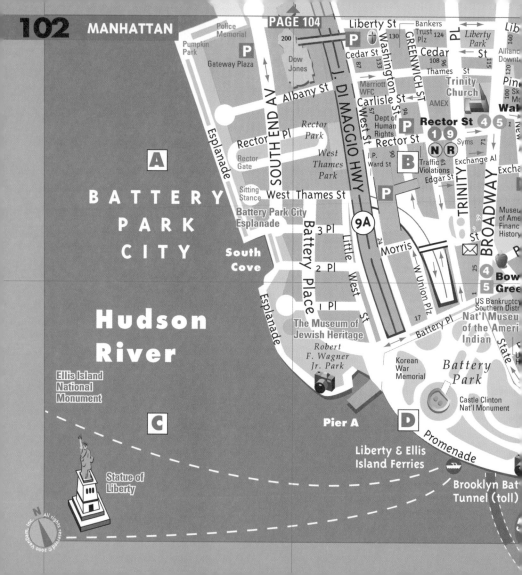

PAGE 104

Police Memorial
Pumpkin Park
Gateway Plaza
Dow Jones

Liberty St
Bankers Trust Plz 124
Lib
Liberty Park
St
Cedar 108
Alliance Downt
115
120
Pin
Sk
100
Mc
Wal

Cedar St 87
Albany St
Carlisle St 94
West St
Dept of Human Rights
Rector St
J.P. 90
Ward St
West Thames Park
West Thames St
Sitting Stance
Battery Park City Esplanade

Washington St 133
Greenwich St 130
Thames St 96
Marriott WFC
AMEX
Trinity Church

Rector St 4 5 1
1 9
Syms 71
N R
Traffic Violations 9
Edgar St
Exchange Al
Exch

South End Av
Rector Pl
Rector Park
Rector Gate
West Thames Park

A

B A T T E R Y
P A R K
C I T Y

South Cove

Hudson River

Ellis Island National Monument

C

Esplanade

Battery Place
3 Pl
2 Pl
1 Pl
The Museum of Jewish Heritage
Robert F. Wagner Jr. Park

Little West St
9A
Morris
W Union Plz
17
Battery Pl
24

St
39
TRINITY
BROADWAY
Museu of Ame Financ History

25
4 5
Bow
Gree
US Bankruptcy Southern Distr
Nat'l Museu of the Ameri Indian

Korean War Memorial
Battery Park
Castle Clinton Nat'l Monument

Pier A

D

Promenade

Liberty & Ellis Island Ferries

Statue of Liberty

Brooklyn Bat Tunnel (toll)

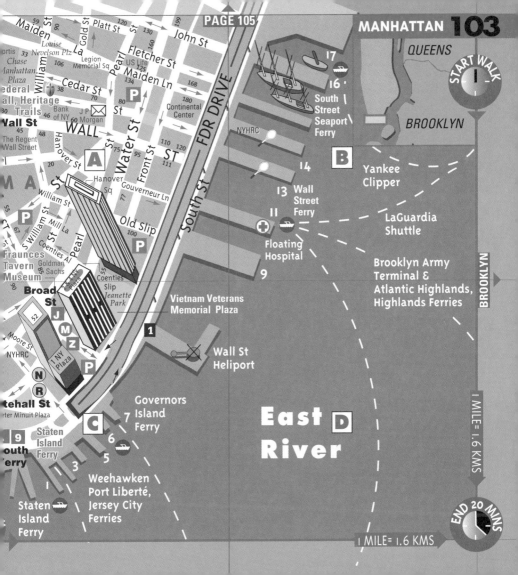

QUEENS

START WALK
1

BROOKLYN

Maiden St 59
Gold St 90
Platt St 120
130
John St 160 199

ortis 33 Louise Nevelson Plz
Chase Manhattan Plaza 106
Fletcher St
Pearl 125
US Lite

Cedar St 38
Maiden Ln 134
168

ederal all, Heritage Trails
70
St 180
Continental Center

Bank of NY 60
J P Morgan 46

Wall St 45
48
The Regent Wall Street

WALL ST

110
111
95
120

Hanover St 20

A

Water St
Front St

NYHRC

B

Yankee Clipper

17

16

South Street Seaport Ferry

14

13   Wall Street Ferry

11

LaGuardia Shuttle

Hanover Sq
Gouverneur Ln

William St
55
57

P

67

S William St
Mill La

Coenties Al
Pearl

Old slip
100

Floating Hospital

9

Brooklyn Army Terminal & Atlantic Highlands, Highlands Ferries

Fraunces Tavern Museum
Goldman & Sachs 90
55 1 NY Plaza

Coenties Slip
Jeanette Park

Vietnam Veterans Memorial Plaza

1

BROOKLYN

Broad St

52

J

M
Z

1 NY Plaza

P

Moore St

NYHRC

N

R

tehall St
ter Minuit Plaza

C

Wall St Heliport

Governors Island Ferry

7

6

5

East D
River

9 South erry

Staten Island Ferry

3

Staten Island Ferry

Weehawken Port Liberté, Jersey City Ferries

1 MILE= 1.6 KMS

END 20 MINS

1 MILE= 1.6 KMS

PAGE 106

TRIBECA

Finn Square

124
191

Leonard St

Knitting Factory

NY Law School

N Moore St

Franklin St

Chanterelle

Hudson St

107

88
366

355

64

WORTH ST

88

62

Bell Atlantic

BROADWAY

74 The Odeon

Thomas St

40

Trimble Pl

311

Harrison St

Independence Plaza

Jay St

Staple St

Duane Park

Bouley Bakery

Duane St

124

Stuyvesant HS

B

CIV

Tribeca Performing Arts Center

Tribeca Bridge

Tribeca Park

Reade St

46

71

Chamb

A

North Esplanade

CHAMBERS ST

1 WTC

160

Chambers St

160

CT

The Real World Rockefeller Pavilion Park

Park House

End Av

Warren St

Windows on the World Greatest Bar on Earth

CHAMBERS ST

95

143

102

269

City Ha

138

132

81

2

A C

285

3

9

Esplanade

River Terrace

Play ground

Lilly Pool

Park Pl West

College of Insurance

2 WTC

Observation Deck

Greenwich St

Warren St

Il Giglio 67

WEST

126

57

2

S Flan

West St

J. DIMAGGIO HWY

Boro of Manhattan CC

Murray St

Murray St

253

62

41

109

9A

World Trade Center

U.S. Customs

Park Pl

21

47

2

3

Park Pl

Woolwo Bldg

Kinney Shoe Co

219

Barclay St

WFC

W T C

C

Mercantile Exchange

Vesey

Merrill Lynch

Amex

Lehman Bros

7 WTC

6 WTC

Vesey St

Borders

5 WTC

WTC

Vesey St

C

St. Paul's Chapel

N

E

Belvedere

WFC Plaza

Winter Garden

Manhattan Sailing School

Merrill Lynch

D

Millenium Hilton

Fulton St

Dey St

Century 21

R

Ferries to Hoboken, Liberty Science Ctr & State Park

C

North Cove

World Financial Center

S End Av

225

3 WTC Marriott Hotel

Vesey St

4 WTC Commodities Exch.

Cortlandt St

Cortlandt St

One Liberty Plaza

NYL Care Health Plans

Cortlandt St

1

9

Liberty Pl

Pumpkin Park

Police Memorial

Liberty St

Bankers Trust Plz

124

Liberty Park

Hudson River

P

Gateway Plaza

Dow Jones

200

Cedar

87

Washington St

130

Greenwich St

Thames St

Trinity Pl

333

108

96

St

120

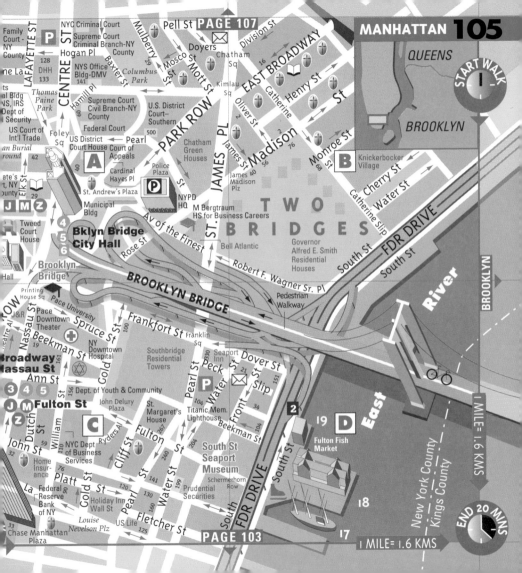

PAGE 107

QUEENS

BROOKLYN

START WALK

Family Court - NY County

NYC Criminal Court

Supreme Court Criminal Branch-NY County

Hogan Pl

Pell St

Doyers

Mosco St

Chatham Sq

Division St

ne La Fayette

128

DHH

133

NYS Office Bldg-DMV 141

Columbus Park

Kimlau Sq

EAST BROADWAY

16

Catherine

Henry St

St

ts al Bldg NS, IRS Dept of Security

60

Hamill Pl

Supreme Court Civil Branch-NY County

U.S. District Court– Southern

Oliver St

2

Madison

2

76

Monroe St

68

Knickerbocker Village

Cherry St

US Court of Int'l Trade

Federal Court

US District Court House

Pearl Court of Appeals

500

James St

James St

56

B

Water St

an Burial round

42

St. Andrew's Plaza

A

Cardinal Hayes Pl

Police Plaza

Chatham Green Houses

James & Madison Plz

140

TWO

Catherine slip

J M Z

Municipal Bldg

NYPD HQ

M Bergtraum HS for Business Careers

BRIDGES

FDR DRIVE

Tweed Court House

4 5 6

Bklyn Bridge City Hall

Av of the Finest

Bell Atlantic

Governor Alfred E. Smith Residential Houses

South St

South St

Hall

Brooklyn Bridge

Rose St

Robert F. Wagner Sr. Pl

River

BROOKLYN

Printing House Sq

Pace University

BROOKLYN BRIDGE

Pedestrian Walkway

J&R

Nassau St

Pace Downtown Theater

Spruce St

Frankfort St

Franklin Sq

Beekman St

19

NY Downtown Hospital

100

Southbridge Residential Towers

Seaport Inn

Dover St

East

Broadway Nassau St

161

Gold St

Peck Slip

Water St

21

30

151

Ann St

Pearl St

Slip

3 4 5

156

Dept. of Youth & Community

John Delury Plaza

104

Front St

34

2

J M Z

Fulton St

St. Margaret's House

Titanic Mem. Lighthouse

Beekman St

104

19

D

Dutch St

William

110

C

NYC Dept of Business Services

Ryders Al

Fulton St

287

204

Fulton Fish Market

John St

59

32

Home Insur- ance

76

Platt St

Cliff St

Water St

240

South St Seaport Museum

Schermerhorn Row

South St

18

La

Federal Reserve Bank of NY

Gold St

120

141

199

Prudential Securities

Louise Nevelson Plz

Holiday Inn Wall St

Pearl St

130

Water St

Fletcher St

New York County

Kings County

33

Chase Manhattan Plaza

US Life

125

PAGE 103

South St

FDR DRIVE

17

1 MILE = 1.6 KMS

1 MILE=1.6 KMS

END 20 MINS

29

Elk St

40

Thomas Paine Park

Baxter St

Mulberry St

Mott St

Centre St

Lafayette St

PARK ROW

JAMES PL

St

Foley Sq

Pearl St

Beekman St

John St

Broadway

Cliff St

Platt St

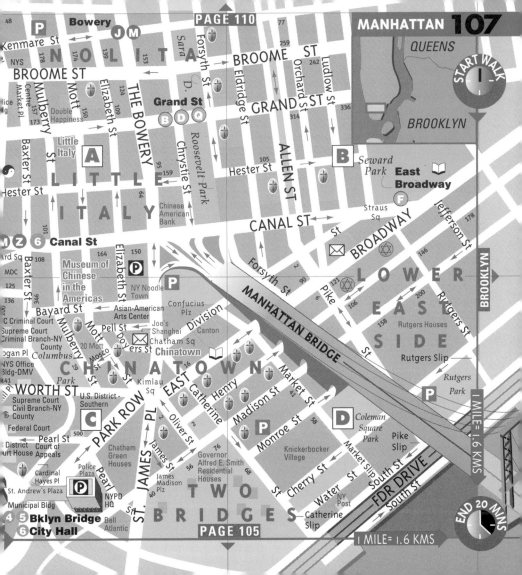

PAGE 112

W 10 St
Weehawken St
649
Christopher St 148
St Luke's-in-the-Field
Wings 656
The
Archive
447

Barrow St
149

617
Morton St 594 620
90
Printing House Fitness & Racquet

46
45
42
40

West St

Leroy St 144 598
FedEx
603

Clarkson St 588

560 Wash. 517

WEST HOUSTON

310 Sa
567 Tu
Co

GREENWICH ST

HUDSON

464

Washington St

St. John's Bldg

UPS Terminal

Port Autho

471
301

A

P

9A

B

C

D

Hudson River

Hudson River Park

Holland Tunnel to NJ

78

34

32

JOE DIMAGGIO HWY

CANAL

Wat

© 1998 Vista, Inc. All rights reserved

PAGE 114
PAGE 109
PAGE 107

Jones Al
Bleecker St
Bleecker St
6
Broadway Lafayette St
B D
F Q

Amato Opera

E 2 St

SECOND AV

Anthology Film Archives
Yonah Schimmel
2 Av F

Puck Bldg
Pratt Institute
Jersey St
Pravda

N O H O
BOWERY
Mulberry St
Mott St
Elizabeth St

Peretz Sq
FIRST AV
Russ & Daughters
Katz's Deli

Mekka
Mercury Lounge
E HOUSTO

AV A
AV B
AV R

Ludlow St
Essex St
Norfolk St
Suffolk St
The Bank

A
N O L I T A
Prince St

Chrystie St
Forsyth St
Sara D.

Stanton St
NY School for the Deaf
Eldridge St
Allen St
Orchard St
Baby Jupiter
Arlene Grocery

B
L O H O

Freeman Al

Spring St
6

P
L I T T L E
I T A L Y
Spring St

Off-Soho Suites Hotel

Arts at University Settlement
Rivington St

P
Lansky Lounge
Ratners
J M **Delancey S**
Z F **Essex St**

Cleveland Pl
48 Lombardi's
P
NYS

Kenmare St

J M **Bowery**

Delancey St
Lower East Side Tenement Museum

Roosevelt
Forsyth St
Eldridge St
BROOME ST
Orchard St
Ludlow St
ESSEX ST
Norfolk St
Suffolk St

LAFAYETTE ST
CENTRE ST
Mulberry St
Centre Market Pl
Baxter St
Mott St
Elizabeth St

BROOME ST

GRAND ST
B D Q **Grand St**
Gus's Pickles
Seward

C
Little Italy
Chrystie St

D

Hester St
Hester St
Howard St

Park
Seward Park

East Broadway

C H I N A T O W N
J M
Z 6 **Canal St**
CANAL ST
Chinese American Bank

Forsyth St
Allen St
Division St
Straus Sq
Rutgers St
F

PAGE 107

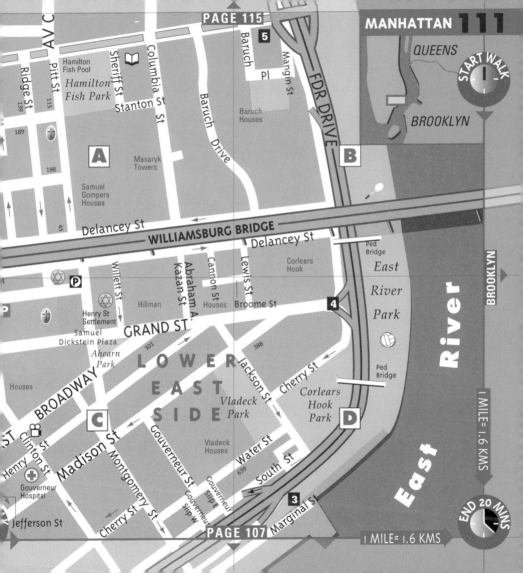

QUEENS

START WALK

BROOKLYN

5

Baruch

Pl

Mangin St

FDR DRIVE

Hamilton Fish Pool

Hamilton Fish Park

Sheriff St

Columbia St

Stanton St

Baruch Drive

Baruch Houses

AV C

Pitt St

Ridge St

139

115

189

198

45

A

Masaryk Towers

Samuel Gompers Houses

B

Delancey St

WILLIAMSBURG BRIDGE

Delancey St

Ped Bridge

East River Park

BROOKLYN

1

P

Willett St

Abraham A. Kazan St

Cannon St

Lewis St

Corlears Hook

P

Henry St Settlement

Samuel Dickstein Plaza

Hillman

Kazan Houses

Broome St

4

GRAND ST.

Ahearn Park

301

L O W E R

388

Jackson St

Cherry St

Ped Bridge

Houses

BROADWAY

E A S T

Vladeck Park

Corlears Hook Park

D

Clinton St

C

S I D E

Vladeck Houses

Water St

South St

East

Henry St

Madison St

Montgomery St

Gouverneur St

Gouverneur Slip E

Gouverneur Slip W

639

River

Gouverneur Hospital

Cherry St

3

1 MILE= 1.6 KMS

Jefferson St

Marginal St

END 20 MINS

1 MILE= 1.6 KMS

PAGE 116

W 14 St Mother

VanDam Bldg   The Cooler

14 St Ⓐ Ⓒ Ⓔ Ⓛ   14 St ①

300   8 Av   Nell's

Chicago B.L.U.E.S.

Jackson Sq

St Vince Hosp

Patisserie Lanciani

Greenwich

MEAT

W 13 St

Fressen

MARKET

240

Campo

Pastis

Little W 12 St

Florent

West St

Gansevoort St

GREENWICH ST

HUDSON ST

EIGHTH AV

Jason Croy

Bloomfield St

A

Horatio St

B

Wave

W 4 ST

Abingdon Sq

Thea Off P

Jane St

Bleecker St

9A

W 12 St

Biography Bookshop

White Horse Tavern

Bethune St

Westbeth Theater

Bank St

Washington St

W E S T

Eighty Eight's

W 11

V I L L A G E

55 Grove Cabaret

Perry St

Lucille Lortel   Arthur's Tavern

Charles La

Bedford

Charles St

Christopher St

Hudson River

W 10 St

D

Grove Ct

C 48

Weehawken St

Christopher St

Wings   The Archive

St Luke's-in-the-Field

Barrow St

Morton St

Leroy St

JOE DiMAGGIO HWY

West St

PAGE 108

56 / 54 / 53 / 52 / 51 / 50 / 49 / 46 / 45

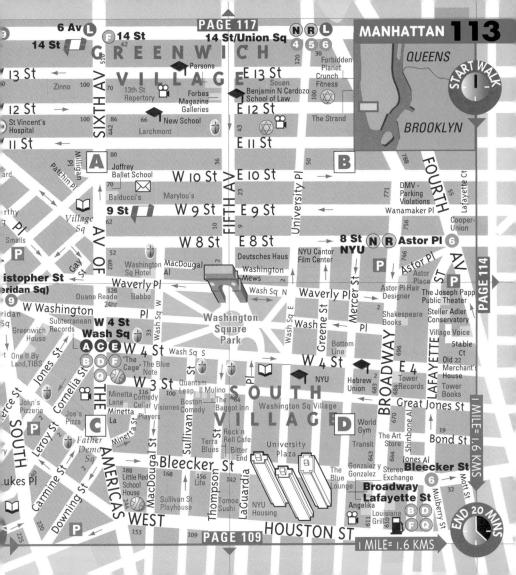

This is a map of Greenwich Village / South Village, Manhattan.

Street labels and points of interest:

6 Av — L
14 St — F — 14 St
N R L
4 5 6 30

QUEENS

START WALK

BROOKLYN

GREENWICH VILLAGE

13 St
Zinno
13th St Repertory
Parsons
E 13 St
Souen
Benjamin N Cardozo School of Law
Forbidden Planet
Crunch Fitness

12 St
St Vincent's Hospital
Forbes Magazine Galleries
New School
Larchmont
E 12 St
E 11 St
The Strand

11 St

Milligan Pl
Patchin Pl

A
Joffrey Ballet School
Balducci's
Marylou's
W 10 St
E 10 St
University Pl
B
DMV - Parking Violations
Wanamaker Pl
FOURTH AV
Lafayette Ct

Village Sq
Smalls
9 St
W 9 St
E 9 St
Cooper-Union

Gay St
W 8 St
E 8 St
8 St NYU
N R — Astor Pl — 6

Christopher St (Sheridan Sq)
Washington Sq Hotel
MacDougal Al
Deutsches Haus
Washington Mews
NYU Cantor Film Center
Astor Pl
Astor Place
PAGE 114

Waverly Pl
Wash Sq N
Waverly Pl
Astor Pl Hair Designer
The Joseph Papp Public Theater

W Washington Pl
Duane Reade 24hr
Babbo
Wash Sq E
Wash Sq
Mercer St
Greene St
Shakespeare Books
Steller Adler Conservatory
Village Voice

W 4 St
Wash Sq
Greenwich House
Subterranean Records
One If By Land, TIBS
Washington Square Park
Wash Sq S
W 4 St
Bottom Line
Pl
Stable Ct
Old Merchant's House
Tower Records

A C E W 4 St
B D F Q
"The Cage"
The Blue Note
W 3 St
NYU
Hebrew Union
Tower Books

Cornelia St
Jones St
John's Pizzeria
Joe's Pizza
C
Father Demo Sq
THE AMERICAS
Quantam Leap
Il Mulino
Minetta Lane
Comedy Cellar
Minetta La
Visiones
Boston Comedy
Players
Sullivan St
The Baggot Inn
SOUTH VILLAGE
Washington Sq Village
D
World Gym
Transit
Great Jones St
Broadway
Bond St
The Art Store
Shinbone Al
Jones Al

Leroy St
Carmine St
Downing St
Bleecker St
Little Red School House
Sullivan St Playhouse
MacDougal St
Thompson St
Terra Blues
Rock'n Roll Cafe
Bitter End
Life
Tomoe Sushi
LaGuardia Pl
University Plaza
NYU Housing
The Blue Lounge
Gonzalez y Gonzalez
Stereo Exchange
Bleecker St
6
Mulberry St
Mott St

WEST
Angelika
NYU Housing
HOUSTON ST
Louisiana Grill
Broadway Lafayette St
B D F Q

1 MILE = 1.6 KMS

END 20 MINS

PAGE 118

L 1 Av

E 14 St

92 | Variety Arts | 106 | Kiel's | 213 | 300 | Agrotikon 350 | 219 | 444 | 500 | 210

NY Eye & Ear Infirmary

E 13 St

100 | CSC Rep | 142 | Airmarket | 246 Ukrainian Museum | 192 | Detour 356 | 198 | 448 | 500 | 550 | 196

E 12 St

FOURTH AV

Webster Hall | 67 | Stuyvesant Al | 242 | Iso | Angelica Kitchen | Brownies | 500 | 546

E 11 St

124 NY Central Art Supply | 232 | Dancespace at St Mark's Church–in–the–Bowery | 158 | Izzy Bar Standard | B | 500 Tompkins Sq | 548

55 | 98 | E 10 St

St Mark's Book Shop | 128 | 145 | 2 Av Deli | Col Legno | Theater for the New City | 147 | Russian & Turkish Baths PS 122 | Alt.Coffee

Wanamaker Pl | 756 | 115 | E 9 St

138 | EAST

Hasaki | Around the Clock | Coney Island High | 134 | Jules

6 Astor Pl

Cooper-Union | Saint Mark's Pl | Alphabets | VILLAGE

Stuyvesant St | McSorley's | 119 | Orpheum | Pearl Theater Co | 115

Astor Pl | PAGE 113 | E 7 St

746 | Astor Wines & Liquors | Joe's Pub | 2 | Taras Shevchenko Pl | 36 | 104 | 48 | 86 | 100 | University of the Streets | 95 | Pyramid Club | 94

Joseph Papp Public Theater | YWCA

E 6 St

Stella Adler Conservatory | 200 | 87 | ALPHABE

Audobon Society | Village Voice | Stable Ct | Cooper Sq | E 5 St | NY Theater Workshop | 300 | Village View Houses | 59 | 74 | Opaline | CITY

Old Merchant's House | 185 | 550 | 56

684 | 44 | Bowery Bar | Duo | La MaMa E.T.C. | 53 | 86 | E 4 St | 130 | Little Rickie | 138 | 50 | First Houses | 180 | 42 | 242 Brisas la Caribe

Fez | Great

Jones St

Jean Cocteau Rep | C | Internet Cafe | D | Context

670 | Bouwerie Lane Theater | 19 | Bond St

Shinbone Al | 644 | Jones Al | NOHO | E 2 St | 42 | 86 | 13 | Mekka

SoHo St | Crosby St | Bleecker St | Amato Opera | Extra Pl | Anthology Film Archives | Mercury Lounge | 225

6 | 32 | Mott St | CBGB | Yonah Schimmel | Peretz Sq | The Bank

Broadway Lafayette St | Elizabeth St | BOWERY | 2 Av | F | EAST HOUSTON ST | Orchard St | 207 | Ludlow St | Essex St | Norfolk St | Suffolk St | 151

B D | 73 | 208

F Q

PAGE 110

Tompkins Square Park

E A S T

© 2000 MapQuest.com, Inc. All rights reserved

QUEENS

START WALK

BROOKLYN

East

River

East
River
Park

FDR

DRIVE

6

A

B

5

C

D

Jacob Riis
Houses

Jacob Riis
Houses

Lillian Wald
Houses

Baruch
Houses

La Plaza
Cultural
Community
Garden

Hamilton
Fish Pool

Hamilton
Fish Park

yorican
ts Cafe

Szold Pl

AV C

AV D

Ridge St

Pitt St

Sheriff St

Columbia St

Baruch Dr

Baruch
Pl

Mangin St

Stanton St

St

th & B

P

P

700
213
199
198
700
740
654
147
650
162
394
145
448
134
650
126
107
90
90
77
60
700
301
752
41
300
33
360
1
139
115

1 MILE= 1.6 KMS

END 20 MINS

1 MILE= 1.6 KMS

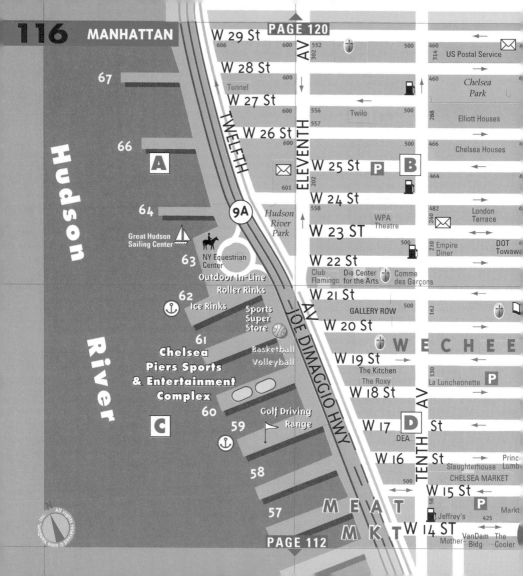

PAGE 120

Hudson River

TWELFTH AV

ELEVENTH AV

9A

Tunnel

W 29 St
W 28 St
W 27 St
W 26 St
W 25 St
W 24 St
W 23 ST
W 22 St
W 21 St
W 20 St
W 19 St
W 18 St
W 17 St
W 16 St
W 15 St
W 14 ST

67
66
64
63
62
61
60
59
58
57

A
B
C
D

Great Hudson Sailing Center
NY Equestrian Center
Outdoor In-Line Roller Rinks
Ice Rinks
Sports Super Store
Chelsea Piers Sports & Entertainment Complex
Basketball Volleyball
Golf Driving Range

Hudson River Park

Twilo

WPA Theatre

Club Flamingo
Dia Center for the Arts
Comme des Garçons

GALLERY ROW

W E C H E E

The Kitchen
The Roxy
La Luncheonette

DEA

Slaughterhouse
Princ Lumb
CHELSEA MARKET

Jeffrey's
Markt

Mother-
VanDam Bldg
The Cooler

JOE DiMAGGIO HWY

TENTH AV

US Postal Service
Chelsea Park
Elliott Houses
Chelsea Houses
London Terrace
DOT Towawa
Empire Diner

552
606
600
600
600
601
558
460
314
460
288
466
464
482
240
210
202
552
557
557
556
500
500
500
500
500
500
500
302
162
130
58
425

M E A T
M K T

© 2000 VarUSA, Inc. All rights reserved

QUEENS

START WALK

BROOKLYN

Catch A Rising Star
P

Fashion Institute of Technology
FIT - Haft Auditorium
Goodman Resource Center

enn Ststion uth Houses

American Jewish

164 Currican
28 St
① ⑨

Ubu Repertory

TADA!
28 St Theatre

Brecht Forum

F L O W E R

M A R K E T

W 26 St

B

Madison Square Park

F A S H I O N

D I S T R I C T

A
High School of Fashion Industries

P

Chelsea Antiques Market P

W 24 St

Worth Sq

SIXTH AV

BWY

McBurney YMCA

C E 23 St
① ⑨ **23 St**

Chelsea Hotel, Serena

Chelsea Savoy

F **23 St**

St Martin's Press

N R **23 St**

Flatiron Bldg

BWY

C H E L S E A

Bright Food Shop

eter's ch

Atlantic

Joyce Theater

Chelsea Int'l Youth Hostel

Rocking Horse Cafe Mexicano

Dance Theater Workshop

Irish Repertory

Gotham Comedy Club Ohm

Cheetah
Periyali P
Caffe Bondi

Metronome

E 20 St

AV OF THE AMERICAS

Gauntlet

F L A T I R O N

E 19 St

Hackers, Hitters & Hoops
v Holtzbrink

Bed Bath & Beyond

① ⑨ **18 St**

Poster America

Barnes & Noble Exec. Offices

E 18 St

Judy's Chelsea

C

Rebar

Authority Bldg

St Vincent's Cancer Center

EIGHTH AV

SEVENTH AV

Actor's Playhouse

NY Foundling Hospital

D
SoHo Arts Group

Disney

E 17 St
Sale Paragon Annex
Union Square Cafe

FIFTH AV

1 MILE = 1.6 KMS

YIVO Institute for Jewish Research

Paul Smith
P
Mesa Grill

E 16 St

Coffee Shop

E 15 St

El Cid

stead

14 St **A C E L** 8 Av

262

NY State Armory

① ② ③ ⑨ **14 St**

P
14 St

6 Av **L**

F **14 St**

E 14

END 20 MINS

1 MILE = 1.6 KMS

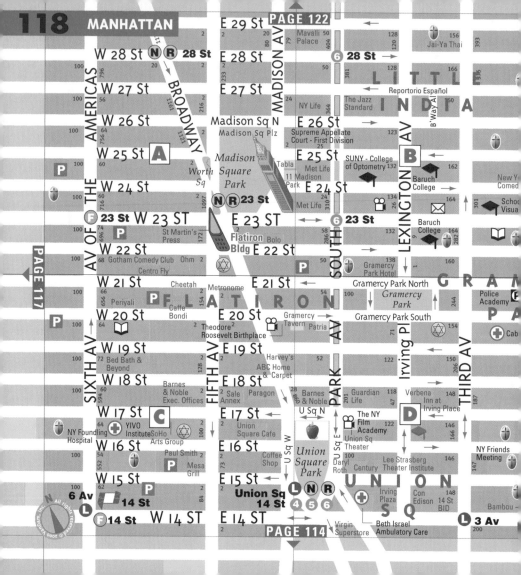

PAGE 122

PAGE 117

PAGE 114

E 29 St

W 28 St **Ⓝ Ⓡ** 28 St   E 28 St   Mavalli Palace   **6** 28 St   Jai-Ya Thai

W 27 St   E 28 St

BROADWAY

W 27 St   E 27 St   Reportorio Español

AMERICAS

W 26 St   NY Life   The Jazz Standard

Madison Sq N   E 26 St   LITTLE INDIA

Madison Sq Plz   B'Way A

W 25 St **A**   Supreme Appellate Court - First Division   SUNY - College of Optometry

Worth Sq   Madison Square Park   Tabla   SUNY - College of Optometry   **B**

W 24 St   Met Life   11 Madison Park   E 24 St   Baruch College

F 23 St W 23 ST   **Ⓝ Ⓡ** 23 St   E 23 ST   Met Life   **6** 23 St   Baruch College

AV OF THE

W 22 St   St Martin's Press   Flatiron Bldg   E 22 St   Bolo

W 22 St   Gotham Comedy Club   Ohm   Gramercy Park Hotel

W 21 St   Cheetah   Metronome   Gramercy Park North   Gramercy Park   Police Academy

Periyali   Caffe Bondi   Gramercy Park   GRAM

W 20 St   E 20 St   Gramercy Tavern   Patria   Gramercy Park South   Cab

Theodore Roosevelt Birthplace

W 19 St   E 19 St   Harvey's   PARK AV

Bed Bath & Beyond   ABC Home & Carpet

W 18 St   Barnes & Noble Exec. Offices   E 18 St   Paragon   Barnes & Noble   Guardian Life   Verbena   Inn at Irving Place

FIFTH AV   Sale Annex   THIRD AV

SIXTH AV   W 17 St **C**   E 17 St   U Sq N   The NY Film Academy

NY Foundling Hospital   YIVO Institute   SoHo Arts Group   Union Square Cafe

W 16 St   E 16 St   Union Square Park   Union Sq Theater

Paul Smith   Coffee Shop   Daryl Roth   Lee Strasberg Theater Institute   NY Friends Meeting

W 15 St   Mesa Grill   E 15 St   Century

6 Av   W 14 St   Union Sq 14 St   **Ⓛ Ⓝ Ⓡ**   Irving Plaza   Con Edison   14 St BID   Bambou

L   **4 5 6**

F 14 St   W 14 ST   E 14 ST   **L** 3 Av

Beth Israel Ambulatory Care

Virgin Superstore   PAGE 114

New Y Comed

Schoo Visua

UNION SQ

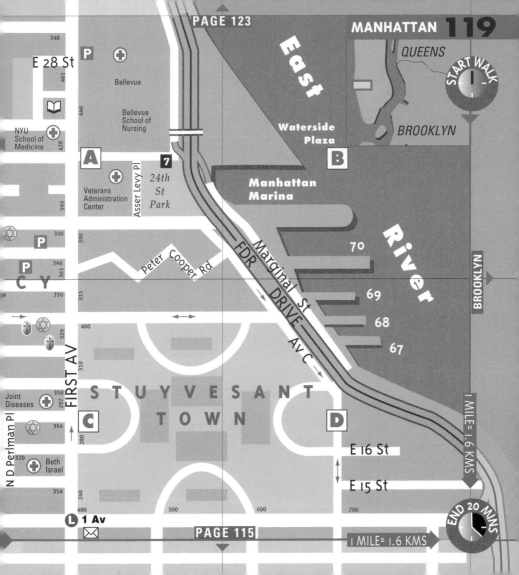

QUEENS

START WALK

BROOKLYN

East River

Waterside Plaza

Manhattan Marina

348

E 28 St

461

P

Bellevue

446

Bellevue School of Nursing

NYU School of Medicine

429

A

7

24th St Park

Veterans Administration Center

Asser Levy Pl

350

P

390

P 346

361

C **Y**

350

315

Peter Cooper Rd

FDR DRIVE

Marginal St

Av C

70

69

68

67

329

400

310

FIRST AV

S T U Y V E S A N T

T O W N

Joint Diseases

350

297

C

354

280

N D Perlman Pl

320

Beth Israel

D

E 16 St

E 15 St

354

240

400

500

600

700

L 1 Av

BROOKLYN

I MILE= 1.6 KMS

END 20 MINS

I MILE= 1.6 KMS

PAGE 124

W 44 St →

Circle Line

Market Diner

Patents 521 W. 43rd

Actors Studio

Westside Theater

400

W 43 St

Judith Anderson, Harold Clurman

Douglas Fairbanks

Playwrights Horizons

400

W 42 St

ELEVENTH AV

John Houseman

Nat Horne

Theater

Lincoln Tunnel to NJ Meadowlands; Giants Stadium; Continental Airline Arena

Martin Kaufman Fed Ex

Signature

CUNY Hunter College

Chez Josephine

W 41 St

Cardinal Stepinac Pl

9A

Greyhound-Trailways Bus Lines

Lincoln

Parking Ramp

B

W 40 St →

To NJ 495

Galvin Av

NY Waterway

W 39 St

Tunnel

P

DOT Towaway Lot

W 38 St →

P

81

Javits Convention Center

W 37 St ←

78

W 36 St ←

DYER AV

76

W 35 St ←

P

W 34 St ↔

The Original Improv

JOE DIMAGGIO HWY

W 33 St ←

73

Daily News, WNET Channel 13

D

Lincoln Tunnel Entrance

W 32 St ↔

72

30 St Heliport

W 31 St

Hudson River

W 30 St

TWELFTH AV

ELEVENTH AV

TENTH AV

W 29 St

PAGE 116

W 44 St · Cornell Club

PAGE 126

Princeton Club · Century Club · Berkeley College · Campbell Apt

P · W 43 St

Condé Nast Tower, ACLU · Laura Belle · HBO · Grace Bldg · NYU Midtown Center · Nat Sherman · E 43 St · Grand Central & 34 St Partnership

Graybar Bldg

Archbishop F. J. Sheen P

B **D** **F** **Q** **42 St (Bryant Park)**

W 42 ST

Bell Atlantic

Chrysler Bldg · Xerc

4 **5** **6** **7** **S**

Grand Hyatt Hotel

i

7 E 42 ST · 5 Av

Bryant Park

A

NY Public Library · Republic National Bank

W 41 St · E 41 St

Helmsley Spear · Whitney Museum · Philip Morris · Shuttle buses

Philips Electronics

Grand Central

Gruner & Jahr · Mobil · NY He

NY Hel

Empire Blue Cross & Blue Shield

B

M I D T O W

W 40 St · E 40 St

Broadway

39 St · E 39 St

Doral Park Av · "W" Tuscany · "W" Court

P

W 38 St · Lord & Taylor · E 38 St

Morgans, Asia de Cuba · Kitano

Shelburne

E A S T

W 37 St · E 37 St

Morgan Library

Sheraton Russell

W 36 St · E 36 St

33 St · **34 St** · Metro · Greater NY Chamber of Commerce · E 35 St

Science Industry & Business Library (SIBL)

Sniffen Ct

M U R

Herald Sq

B **D** **N**

Macy's

W 34 ST · **F** **Q** **R**

Greeley Sq

Empire State Bldg

CUNY Graduate Center · E 34 ST

Dumont Plaza Suite

H

33 St **6**

D

W 33 St · Golda Meir Sq · Empire State News

Manhattan Mall · **C** · P The Manhattan

W 32 St · E 32 St · Hangawi · Coach House

St. Francis of Assisi

W 31 St · **K O R E A** · E 31 St

The Roger Williams

LEXINGTON AV

P

THIRD AV

W 30 St · **T O W N** · American Academy of Dramatic Arts · E 30 St

Sim Har

N · All rights reserved

P

W 29 St · SIXTH AV · BWY · FIFTH AV · **PAGE 118** E 29 St

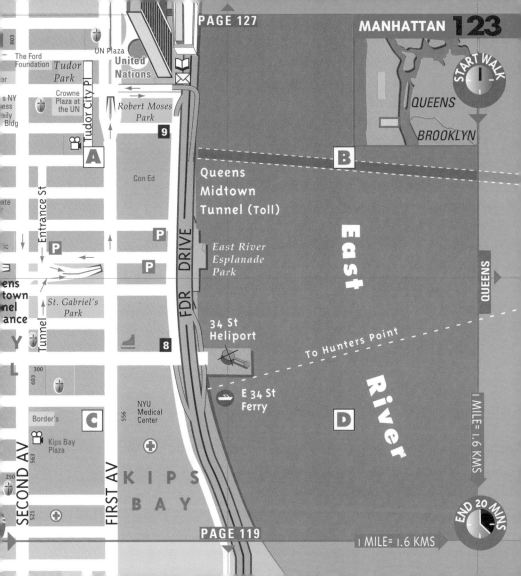

START WALK

QUEENS

BROOKLYN

The Ford Foundation

UN Plaza

Tudor Park

United Nations

Crowne Plaza at the UN

Robert Moses Park

A

9

Tudor City Pl

Con Ed

B

Queens Midtown Tunnel (Toll)

Entrance St

P

P

East River Esplanade Park

P

FDR DRIVE

E a s t

St. Gabriel's Park

ens town nel ance

Y

L

Tunnel

34 St Heliport

8

To Hunters Point

E 34 St Ferry

QUEENS

300

603

R i v e r

D

Border's

C

NYU Medical Center

556

Kips Bay Plaza

563

SECOND AV

FIRST AV

K I P S

B A Y

250

521

1 MILE = 1.6 KMS

END 20 MINS

1 MILE = 1.6 KMS

PAGE 128

Copacabana

W 57 ST John Jay College
806 CBS 600 500

96

Days Looking Inn Glass
852

95

W 56 St
798 P 500

HS Environmental Studies
834 400

94

Hudson River Park
780

W 55 St
778 500 P

C L I N T O N

Theater Four
812 400

93

A

9A

De Witt Clinton Park
760

W 54 St
758 AT & T 500 B 792 400

92

NYC Convention Pier

W 53 St
738 Ensemble Studio Theatre 766 400

Hudson

W 52 St
722 Irish Arts Center 500

(W.C. Handy Pl) 400
St Clare's Hospital
750

90

River

700 600
680 600

W 51 St
706 500

714

THEA

W 50 St
684

660 600

W 49 St
666

500
HS of Graphic Communication Arts 500

DIST

640 600

W 48 St

86

620 600

W 47 St
628

Hell's Kitchen Park
646

400

Intrepid Sea-Air-Space Museum

600

W 46 St

Pan Asian Theater
664 400
→ Repertory

580 600

W 45 St
610

H E L L ' S
638 400

84

C

560 600

W 44 St
592

K I T C H E N
D

New Dramatist

83

JOE DIMAGGIO HWY
TWELFTH AV

W 43 St
572 Market Diner
540 600

Patents 500
521 W. 43rd

Actors Studio

Westside Theater 400
596

ELEVENTH AV

Judith Anderson, Harold Clurman
576

Douglas Fairbanks P

Playwrights Horizons 400

81

Circle Line
520

TENTH AV

554

W 42 ST Theater Row Nat
John Horne
Houseman

PAGE 120
Kaufman Signature 500

Samuel Beckett

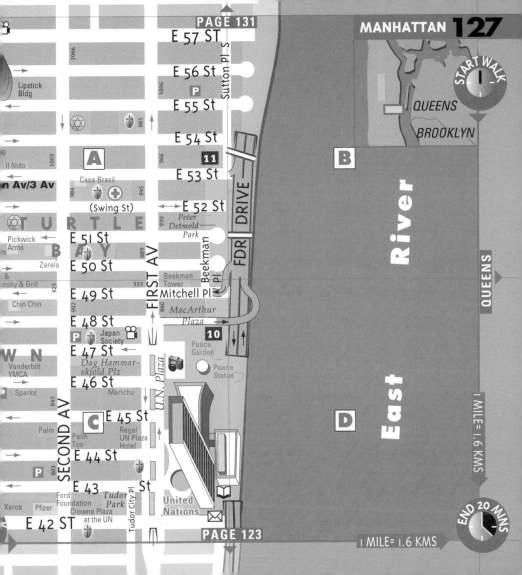

START WALK

QUEENS

BROOKLYN

Lipstick Bldg

Il Nido

A

Casa Brasil

(Swing St)

Av/3 Av

1003

1066

1066

985

984

945

B

930

11

River

Pickwick Arms

Zarela

&
nsky & Grill

Chin Chin

B
A

T U R T L E
B A Y

889

923

FDR DRIVE

Peter Detmold Park

Beekman Tower

Mitchell Pl

MacArthur Plaza

10

Peace Garden

Peace Statue

B

QUEENS

D

East

Beekman Pl

FIRST AV

860

902

Vanderbilt YMCA

Sparks

Palm

W N

P

Japan Society

Dag Hammar-skjold Plz

Marichu

C E 45 St

U.N. Plaza

Palm Too

Regal UN Plaza Hotel

SECOND AV

843

803

P

Xerox   Pfizer

Ford Foundation
Crowne Plaza at the UN

Tudor Park

Tudor City Pl

United Nations

1 MILE= 1.6 KMS

END 20 MINS

E 57 ST
E 56 St
E 55 St
E 54 St
E 53 St
E 52 St
E 51 St
E 50 St
E 49 St
E 48 St
E 47 St
E 46 St
E 44 St
E 43 St
E 42 ST

Sutton Pl S

1 MILE= 1.6 KMS

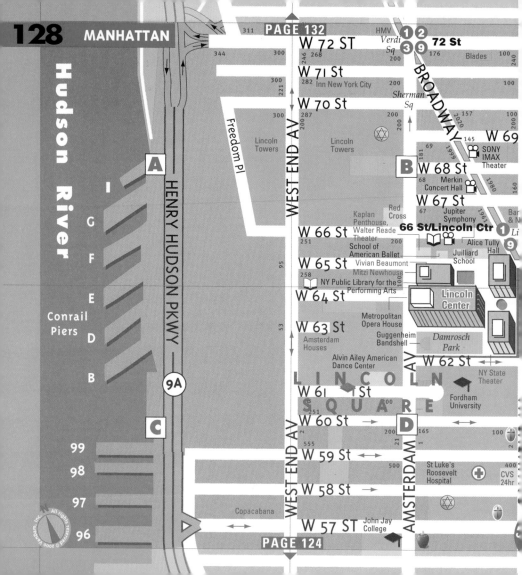

Hudson River

PAGE 132

311

HMV

W 72 ST

Verdi Sq

72 St

344

300

300

246 268

200

176

Blades

100 240

300

W 71 St

282 Inn New York City

200

100

BROADWAY

221

300

W 70 St

Sherman Sq

287

200

200

200

200

157

2020

100 200

Freedom Pl

WEST END AV

Lincoln Towers

Lincoln Towers

69

145

W 69

181

1999

SONY IMAX Theater

A

HENRY HUDSON PKWY

B

W 68 St

1980

160

68

Merkin Concert Hall

1961

I

G

67

W 67 St

Jupiter Symphony

Bar & N

F

Kaplan Penthouse, Walter Reade Theater

Red Cross

66 St/Lincoln Ctr

1

Li

E

95

W 66 St

251

School of American Ballet

200

Alice Tully Hall

9

Conrail Piers

D

W 65 St

Vivian Beaumont

258

Mitzi Newhouse

Juilliard School

NY Public Library for the Performing Arts

W 64 St

B

W 63 St

53

Metropolitan Opera House

Lincoln Center

Amsterdam Houses

Guggenheim Bandshell

Damrosch Park

Alvin Ailey American Dance Center

9A

W 62 ST

NY State Theater

L I N C O L N

W 61 St

00

Fordham University

S Q U A R E

C

251

W 60 St

D

165

100

99

555

21

1

2

98

W 59 St

200

97

500

St Luke's Roosevelt Hospital

400

CVS 24hr

96

W 58 St

Copacabana

W 57 ST

John Jay College

AMSTERDAM AV

WEST END AV

© 2000 Vardon, Inc. All rights reserved

PAGE 124

START WALK 1

QUEENS

BROOKLYN

72 St
B Women's Gate
C
Strawberry Fields
Cherry Hill
Rumsey Playfield
Terrace Drive
Naumburg Bandshell
Central Park
Bowling Green
Mineral Springs Concessions
Singer Lilac Walk
Roller Skating
The Mall
Literary Walk
East Drive

101
Fe
Café Des Artistes
81
A
C e n t r a l
Sheep Meadows

CENTRAL PARK WEST

eum of rican Art
Hall
65
41
P
Tavern on the Green w/the Chestnut Room
P a r k
65 St Transverse
Ballplayers Houses
Heckscher Ballfields
The Carousel
The Dairy

B
E 68 St
E 67 St
E 66 St
Balto
E 65 St
Armani
India House
Chase Manhattan
30
793
26
850
272
40
751

NY Society for Ethical Culture
MCA
W 63 St
West Drive
Center Drive
Chess & Checkers House
Chess Rock
Cat Rock
Rat Rock
Heckscher Playground
Umpire Rock
Puppet House
Wollman Mem. Rink
Central Park Zoo
Wildlife Conservation Center
Children's Gate
The Arsenal

FIFTH AV

E 64 St
Berwind Mansion
E 63 St
Post House
E 62 St
Helmsley-Carlton House
711
830
810
690
22
30

The Mayflower Hotel
Trump Int'l Hotel & Tower
m Plaza
NYIT
Merchants' Gate
C
Columbus Cir
A C 1
B D 9
Columbus Circle
59 St

Maine Memorial
Hallett Nature Sanctuary
Gapstow Bridge
Cop Cot
Simon Bolivar Statue
The Pond
Scholars Gate
Grand Army Plz

5 Av
N R
E 61 St
The Pierre
Barneys NY
E 60 St
Sherry-Netherland
Estee Lauder GM
Vidal Sassoon Bldg

MADISON AV

663
667

1 MILE = 1.6 KMS

Artisans' Gate
CENTRAL PARK SOUTH
Artists' Gate
Essex House
Les Célébrités
Inter Continental
St Moritz
Pulitzer Fountain
The Plaza Hotel
FAO Schwarz
E 59 St
E 58 St
Warner Bros Studio Store
E 57 St

NY Coliseum
Universal News
Le Bar Bat
Newsweek, Coliseum Books
Hard Rock Cafe

SEVENTH AV
N
R 57 St
AV OF THE AMERICAS
B
Wyndham
9-W 57
Bergdorf Goodman
Van Cleef & Arpels
Q 57 St
END 20 MINS

P

PAGE 125

1 MILE = 1.6 KMS

PAGE 130

PAGE 134

PAGE 129

Inventors Gate

Terrace Drive

Naumburg Bandshell

Rumsey Playfield

E 72 ST

E 71 St

Madison Av BID

26 Ralph Lauren 84 100 140

861 737

Frick Collection

20

30 720 Asia Society Paul Mellon House 140 962

17

E 70 St

Singer Lilac Walk

Mineral Springs Concessions

Roller Skating

The Mall

28 50 Union Club 136 701

829

NY School Interior De

Central Park

E 69 St

Spanish Institute

2 20 The Americas Society 58

2870

The Sylvia & Danny Kaye 131 Playhouse 926

68 St/ Hunter College 6

Sheep Meadows

E 68 St

A

East Drive

Literary Walk

B

30 793 Council on Foreign Relations

Hunter College 653

E 67 St

2850 26 772

60 640

7th Regiment Armory

16

Balto

E 66 St

40 Sarah D. Roosevelt 751 Mem House 136 625 China House Gallery/ China Inst. in America

65 St Transverse

Ballplayers Houses

The Carousel

Armani

E 65 St

64

Heckscher Ballfields

The Dairy

India House Chase Manhattan

Plaza Athénée 886

16

Heckscher Playground

Children's Gate

E 64 St

Berwind Mansion 30 711

581

136 Jo Jo Lexington

Center Drive

Chess & Checkers House

The Arsenal

E 63 St

810 22 Post House 690

The MAFCO 56 Lowell 5600

Museum of American Illustration 130 Circus B Q

1

Umpire Rock

Puppet House

Wollman Mem. Rink

E 62 St

Helmsley-Carlton House 673

Sherry The Lehmann Regency 535 Feinstein

136 G Trump P

Hallett Nature Sanctuary

Gapstow Bridge

E 61 St

28 Loew's Aureole 140 The Pierre Barneys NY DK Delmonico 784

C C 17

Cop Cot

The Pond

Scholars' Gate

E 60 St

Calvin Klein Ralph Lauren Sherry- Netherland Crate & Barrel 633

French Institute 501 Florence Gould Hall

N R Lexing

Bloomingdal

Artisans' Gate

i

C

9 W 57

Artists' Gate

Grand Army Plz

Pulitzer Fountain

E 59 St

Estée Lauder Vidal Sassoon 625 Au Bar 500

G M Bldg

4 5 6 59

CENTRAL PARK SOUTH

Essex House 200 Les Célébrités 922

Inter Continental 106

St Moritz

The Plaza Hotel

FAO Schwarz

Argosy

7 AV

W 58 St

200 901 Petrossian

Wyndham

Bergdorf Goodman Van Cleef & Arpels

Warner Bros Studio Store

E 58 St

598 The Four Seasons

PARK AV

475 Le Colonia

6 AV

W 57 ST

B Q 57 St

E 57 ST

NikeTown Tourneau

Borders

Hammacher Schlemmer

5 Av N R

FIFTH AV

MADISON AV

LEXINGTON AV

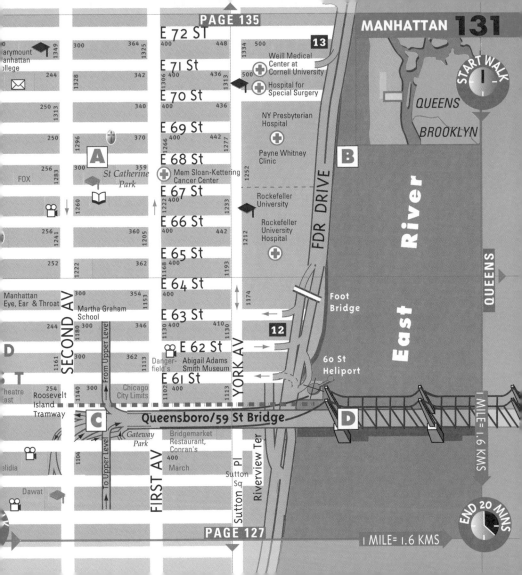

E 72 ST

E 71 ST

E 70 ST

E 69 ST

E 68 ST

E 67 ST

E 66 ST

E 65 ST

E 64 ST

E 63 ST

E 62 ST

E 61 ST

START WALK

QUEENS

BROOKLYN

13

Weill Medical Center at Cornell University

Hospital for Special Surgery

NY Presbyterian Hospital

Payne Whitney Clinic

Mem Sloan-Kettering Cancer Center

Rockefeller University

Rockefeller University Hospital

A

B

D

FDR DRIVE

East River

QUEENS

Foot Bridge

60 St Heliport

12

arymount anhattan ollege

1349

1325

300

364

1328

244

342

1306

400

448

1334

500

500

1313

250

340

1296

250

370

1266

400

442

1277

256

359

FOX

300

1252

1222

400

1233

256

360

1241

1205

252

362

1168

400

1193

1174

Manhattan Eye, Ear & Throat

300

354

1161

1153

SECOND AV

Martha Graham School

244

346

1180

300

1130

400

1130

300

362

1102

400

1113

St Catherine Park

FOX

D

Danger-field's

Abigail Adams Smith Museum

YORK AV

Manhattan Eye, Ear & Throat

Roosevelt Island Tramway

254

1140

300

Chicago City Limits

C

Gateway Park

Bridgemarket Restaurant, Conran's

FIRST AV

From Upper Level

To Upper Level

1104

400

March

Sutton Pl

Sutton Sq

Riverview Ter

Queensboro/59 St Bridge

D

heatre ast

olidia

Dawat

1 MILE= 1.6 KMS

END 20 MINS

1 MILE= 1.6 KMS

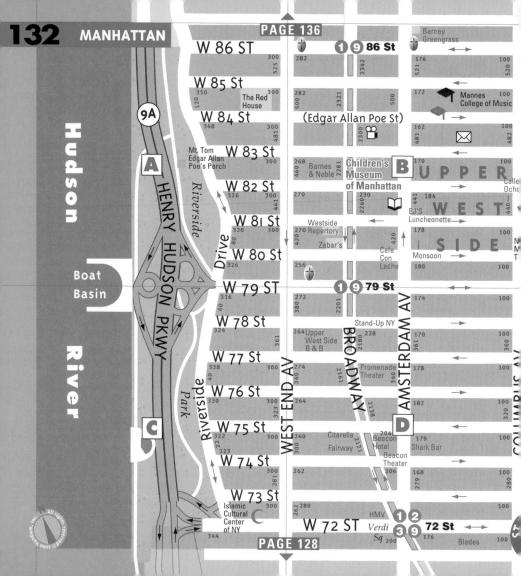

PAGE 136

Hudson River

Boat Basin

HENRY HUDSON PKWY

Riverside Drive

Riverside Park

W 86 ST
W 85 St
W 84 St
W 83 St
W 82 St
W 81 St
W 80 St
W 79 ST
W 78 St
W 77 St
W 76 St
W 75 St
W 74 St
W 73 St
W 72 ST

(Edgar Allan Poe St)

The Red House

Mt. Tom
Edgar Allan
Poe's Perch

Barnes & Noble

Children's Museum of Manhattan

Westside Repertory
Zabar's
Cafe Con Leche

Stand-Up NY

Upper West Side B & B

Promenade Theater

Citarella
Fairway

Beacon Hotel
Beacon Theater

Islamic Cultural Center of NY

Verdi Sq

Barney Greengrass

86 St

Mannes College of Music

UPPER WEST SIDE

EJ'S Luncheonette

Monsoon

79 St

Shark Bar

72 St

Blades

HMV

WEST END AV
BROADWAY
AMSTERDAM AV
COLUMBUS AV

1 9 86 St
1 9 79 St
1 9 72 St
1 2 3 9 72 St

9A

A B C D

PAGE 128

© 2000 Vistar, Inc. All rights reserved

85 St Transverse

START WALK
1

QUEENS

BROOKLYN

86 St B C
2

Mariners'
Gate

Central
Park Precinct
Ross
Pinetum

South
Gatehouse

A

241
2

h of St.
ew & St.
ny

221
2

The
Great
Lawn

Bridle
Path

Cleopatra's
Needle

B

E 82 St

Goethe
House

28
1090

45

1010
2

81 St
Museum of
tural History

se Center
& Space 2

Hunters'
Gate

Delacorte
Theatre

Metropolitan
Museum
of Art

Campbell
Funeral Chapel

1075

E 81 St

36
990

30

B
C
2

Henry Luce
Nature
Observatory

Turtle
Pond

Shakespeare
Garden
Belvedere
Castle

East Drive

West Drive

The Stanhope

E 80 St

(Museum Mile)

1033

PAGE 134

Swedish
Cottage

79 St Transverse

E 79 ST

rican Museum
atural History

Winter
Drive

Central

Cedar Hill

Miners'
Gate

James B
Duke House

French
Embassy

970

E 78 St
2

993

New-York
Historical
Society

Park

Levin
Playground

The Mark

E 77 St

50

170
2

950
2

tral Park West
t Historic Dist

Ladies
Pavillion

Alice in
Wonderland
Statue

76 Street
Gate

E 76 St

MADISON AV

San
Remo
Bldg

The
Ramble

Park View
at the Boathouse

Harkness
House

Daniel
Surrey

30

151
2

C

Loeb
Boathouse

Kerbs Mem.
Model
Boathouse

E 75 St

1 MILE= 1.6 KMS

The
Lake

D

Conser-
vatory
Water

Whitney
Museum
of American Art

E 74

FIFTH AV

The
Dakota

Bow
Bridge

Hans Christian
Andersen Statue

E 73 St

2
121

B

Pilgrim Hill

910
2

28

72 St
C

Women's
Gate

Strawberry
Fields

Cherry
Hill

Wagner's
Cove

Navy
Fountain

Bethesda
Terrace

Inventors'
Gate

E 72 ST

34

CENTRAL PARK WEST

END 20 MINS

1 MILE= 1.6 KMS

85 St Transverse

Central Park Precinct
Ross Pinetum

P

South Gatehouse

Ancient Playground

The Great Lawn

A

Metropolitan Museum of Art

Bridle Path

Cleopatra's Needle

Delacorte Theatre

Henry Luce Nature Observatory
Shakespeare Garden
Belvedere Castle
Swedish Cottage
Winter Drive

Turtle Pond

79 St Transverse

Cedar Hill

Miners' Gate

James B Duke House

Levin Playground

Central

Park

West Drive

East Drive

Ladies Pavilion

The Ramble

C

Parkview at the Boathouse

Loeb Boathouse

Alice in Wonderland Statue

76 Street Gate

Kerbs Mem. Model Boathouse

Conservatory Water

The Lake

Bow Bridge

Hans Christian Andersen Statue

Pilgrim Hill

Bethesda Fountain
Bethesda Terrace

Cherry Hill

Wagner's Cove

Inventors' Gate

N

E 86 ST
✡ 📹 **86** 4 5

1165 | 48 | 78 | 100 | 128
1030 | | | 1021 |

E 85 ST

1130 | 38 | 74 | 132
1030 | 35 | 1000 | 1248

E 84 ST

1109 | ✝ Church of St. Ignatius Loyola | 132

E 83 ST
Goethe House
1010 | 28 | 72 | 132
1090 | 45 | 960 | 1210

B

E 82 ST
Frank E. Campbell Funeral Chapel
1075 | 72 | 100 | 136
| 941 | |

E 81 ST
The Stanhope
2 | 36 | 30 | 64 | Lewis Spencer Morris House | 126
| | 916 | | 1164

E 80 ST
2 | 40 | 76 | 142
1033 | | 903 | Junior League of the City of NY

E 79 ST
French Embassy
1970 | 82 | 100 | 142
39 | 878 | | 1120

E 78 ST
The Mark
2 | 72 | 138
993 | | 863 | **77 St** 6

E 77 ST
50 | The Carlyle | 86 | Lenox Hill Hospital ✚
950 | Cafe Carlyle w/Bemelman's Bar | 840 | 1080

E 76 ST
Harkness House | Daniel | 30 | 58
| Surrey | | 821

D

E 75 ST
Whitney Museum of American Art
2 | 24 | 100 | 136
930 | 940 | | 1036

E 74 ST
2 | 30 | 58 | 142
921 | | 785 |

E 73 ST
910 | 28 | 34 | 68 | 140
| | 760 | 1004

E 72 ST
Madison Av BID
Ralph Lauren | 84 | 100 | 140

FIFTH AV
MADISON AV
PARK AV
LEXINGTON AV

(Museum Mile)

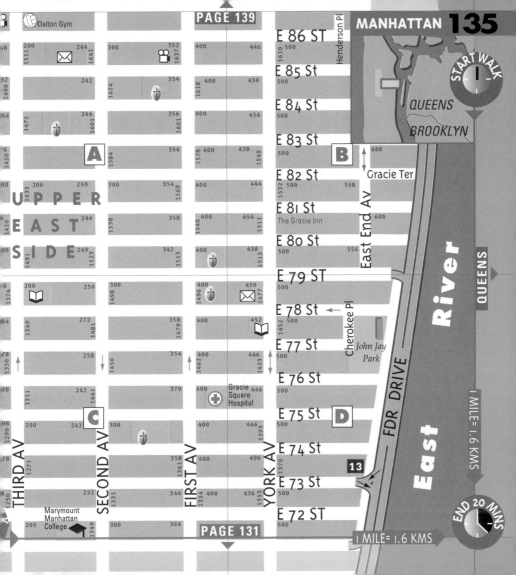

← PAGE 140

W 99 St

Park West

Village

W 98 St

W 97 St

*Riverside
Park*

W 96 ST

A

❶❷❸❾ 96 St

The Latin
Quarter

B

U P P E R

Thalia
Theater
Symphony
Space

Pomander
Walk

W E S T

W 95 St

Joan of Arc
Statue

W 94 St

S I D E

W 93 St

W 92 St

Duane
Reade

Trinity House

Drive W 91 St

← 24hr

(Henry J Brow

Claremont
Riding
Academy

W 90 St

WEST END AV

Soldiers
& Sailors
Monument

W 89 St

BROADWAY

AMSTERDAM AV

W 88 St

D

Barney
Greengrass

W 87 St

COLUMBUS AV

W 86 ST

❶❾ 86 St

W 85 St

The Red
House

Mannes
College of Music

Riverside

HENRY HUDSON PKWY

W 84 St

(Edgar Allan Poe St)

PAGE 132

Hudson

River

9A

North Meadow **PAGE 141**

East Drive

East Meadow

START WALK

QUEENS

BROOKLYN

North Meadow Security Center

97 St Transverse

96 St B C

All Saints † Gate of All Saints

A

Central

Tennis Courts

Park

Woodmen's Gate

B

North Gatehouse

Bridle Path

.5 mi

.25 mi

West Drive

.75 mi

Jackie

Onassis

Reservoir

Fred Lebow Running Track

START FINISH

Engineers' Gate

1.5 mi

CENTRAL PARK WEST

Claremont Stables

C

1 mi

D

1.25 mi

E 95 St

1130 ICP Uptown

E 94 St

2   28   50

FIFTH AV

E 93 St

Jewish 1296   50
Museum

E 92 St

2   30   43

MADISON AV

E 91 St

Cooper–Hewitt
Museum

E 90 St

National Academy
Museum   NY Road
            Runners Club

Fred Lebow Pl

Solomon R   48
Guggenheim
Museum E 88

2   40

PAGE 138

E 87 St

(Museum Mile)

East Drive

86 St B C

Mariners'
Gate

2

241

85 St Transverse

Central
Park Precinct P

Ross
Pinetum

Fred Lebow
Running Track

South
Gatehouse

E 86 ST

2   22

E 85 St

2   28   1130

1030   1130   38

Ancient
Playground

E 84 St

1 MILE= 1.6 KMS

END 20 MINS

PAGE 133

1 MILE= 1.6 KMS

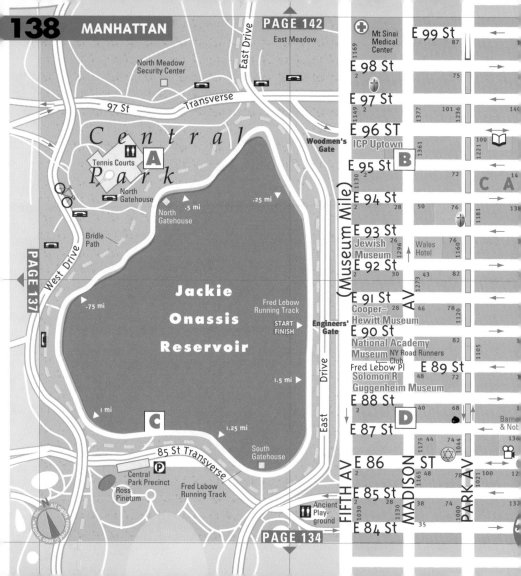

PAGE 142

East Meadow

East Drive

Mt Sinai
Medical
Center

E 99 St 87

E 98 St 75

North Meadow
Security Center

E 97 St 101 1236 140

C e n t r a l

97 St Transverse

E 96 ST
ICP Uptown

Woodmen's
Gate

Tennis Courts
A

Park

E 95 St B

72

C A 14

North
Gatehouse

E 94 St 28 50 76 138

North
Gatehouse

.5 mi .25 mi

E 93 St 26 76
Jewish Wales 1160
Museum Hotel

Bridle
Path

E 92 St 30 43 82

E 91 St 28 46 78
Cooper–
Hewitt Museum 1120

.75 mi

Jackie

Fred Lebow
Running Track

E 90 St
National Academy 82
Museum NY Road Runners 1105
Club
Fred Lebow Pl E 89 St
Solomon R 48 72
Guggenheim Museum

Onassis

START
FINISH

Engineers'
Gate

1.5 mi

E 88 St 40 68
D

Barne
& Not

E 87 St

Reservoir

East

Drive

1 mi

C

1.25 mi

85 St Transverse

South
Gatehouse

E 86 1175 44 74 136
ST 1044

Central
Park Precinct

Ross
Pinetum

Fred Lebow
Running Track

E 85 St 28 38 74 132
1030 1130 1000

Ancient
Play-
ground

E 84 St 35

PAGE 134

West Drive

PAGE 137

(Museum Mile)

FIFTH AV

MADISON

PARK AV

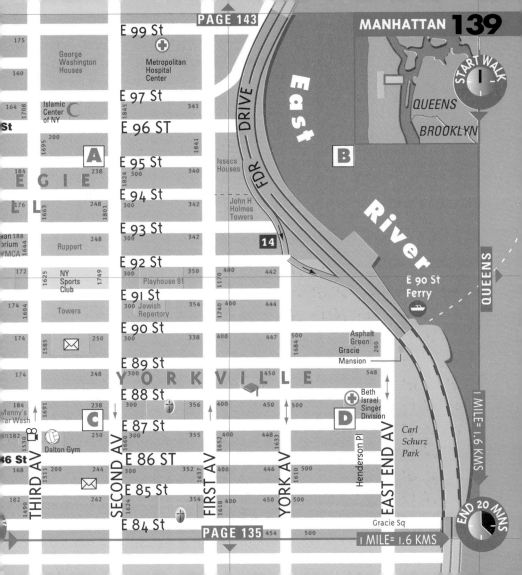

START WALK

QUEENS

BROOKLYN

East

River

FDR DRIVE

George
Washington
Houses

Metropolitan
Hospital
Center

175

160

164
1708

A

B

Islamic
Center
of NY

St

200
1695

E 99 St

E 97 St

E 96 ST

E 95 St

E 94 St

E 93 St

E 92 St

E 91 St

E 90 St

E 89 St

E 88 St

E 87 St

E 86 ST

E 85 St

E 84 St

1845

1824

341

340

342

342

350

354

338

E G I E

184
238

L

176
1663

248
1801

an 188
rium
YMCA

1644

Ruppert

248

172
1625

NY
Sports
Club

1749

Playhouse 91

174
1604

Towers

Issacs
Houses

John H
Holmes
Towers

14

300

300

300

300

300

1170

1740

1841

E 90 St
Ferry

QUEENS

1 MILE = 1.6 KMS

Asphalt
Green
Gracie
Mansion

1684

500
200

174
1585

250

⊠

174

248

Y O R K V I L L E

300

356

355

352

354

184
Manny's
ar Wash

1691

1530

238

in 182

C

250

B

⊡

Dalton Gym

86 St

168
1511

200

244

⊠

182
1490

1624

242

400

400

400

400

400

400

400

450

450

448

446

450

442

444

447

548

Beth
Israel
Singer
Division

450

500

500

500

500

Carl
Schurz
Park

END 20 MINS

THIRD AV

SECOND AV

FIRST AV

1652

1637

1618

YORK AV

1633

1610

Henderson Pl

EAST END AV

Gracie Sq

1 MILE = 1.6 KMS

PAGE 135   454

500

PAGE 144

Hudson River

9A

Henry Hudson Pkwy

Riverside Park

Riverside Drive

W 110 ST ①⑨ CATHEDRAL PKWY ← → Cathedral
Cathedral Pkwy (110 St)

W 109 St
Bloomingdale House Of Music

W 108 St
Nicholas Roerich Museum

W 107 St
Straus Park

A

B

W 106 St

(Duke Ellington Blv

W 105 St

U P P E R

W 104 St
Equity Library Theatre

W E S T

S I D E

W 103 St ← ①⑨ 103 St
NY International American Youth Hostel (AYH)

Frederick Douglass

W 102 St

W 101 St
Trinity Theatre

W 100 St
Men of Fire Memorial

West End Av

Broadway

Amsterdam Av

D

Park

W 99 St

West

W 98 St

Village

W 97 St

W 96 ST ← → ①②③⑨ 96 St

PAGE 136

CENTRAL PARK NORTH

10 St) **B** **C**
348
Douglass Circle

East

Warriors' Gate

2 **3** Farmers' Gate

Charles A. Dana Discovery Center

START WALK

Blockhouse No. 1

Drive

Duck Island

Nutter's Battery Site

Harlem Meer

QUEENS

BROOKLYN

22 | 2

18 | 2

A

West

Lasker Rink & Pool

McGowan's Pass

E 107 St
2 | 48

20 | 2

Strangers' Gate

Huddlestone Bridge

Fort Fish Site

Fort Clinton Site

B

E 106 ST
2 | 26
1550

42 | 2

Great Hill

Drive

The Mount

Conservatory Garden

E 105 St
2

2

The Loch

Ravine

E 104 St
Museum of the City of NY

El Museo del Barrio

20 | 2

The Pool

Central

NY Academy of Medicine

E 103 St
2

03 St **B** **C**
2

20 | 2

Park

Girls' Gate

E 102 St
2 | 22

20 | 2

E 101 St
2 | 20

Boys' Gate

Bridle Path

East Drive

1189

rk

North Meadow

FIFTH AV

Mt. Sinai Medical Center

C

D

1169

est

East Meadow

E 98 St
2

lage

North Meadow Security Center

E 97 St
2

1149

96 St **B** **C**
2

97 St Transverse

Woodmen's Gate

E 96 ST
2

END 20 MINS

Gate of All Saints

Tennis Courts **PAGE 137**

1 MILE= 1.6 KMS

MADISON AV

CENTRAL PARK WEST

MANHATTAN AV

PAGE 142

1 MILE= 1.6 KMS

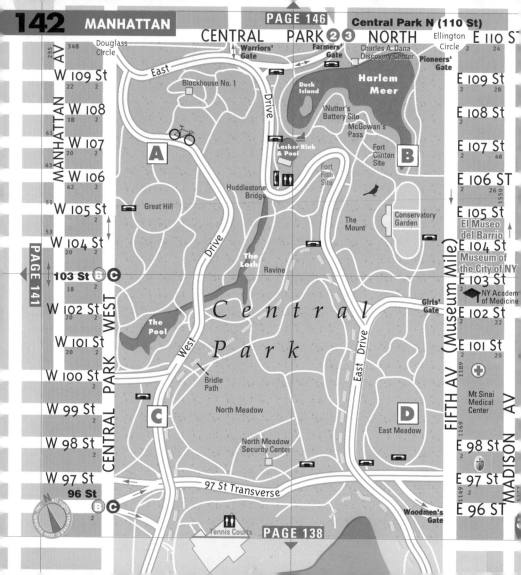

PAGE 146

Central Park N (110 St)

CENTRAL PARK ❷❸ NORTH

Douglass Circle

Ellington Circle

E 110 ST

235 348

Warriors' Gate

Farmers' Gate

Charles A. Dana Discovery Center

Pioneers' Gate

W 109 St

East

Blockhouse No. 1

Duck Island

Harlem Meer

E 109 St

22 2

Drive

W 108

Nutter's Battery Site

McGowan's Pass

E 108 St

18 2

MANHATTAN AV

W 107

Lasker Rink & Pool

Fort Clinton Site

B

E 107 St

20 2

63

A

Fort Fish Site

E 106 ST

W 106

Huddlestone Bridge

26 1550

42 2

51

W 105 St

Great Hill

The Mount

Conservatory Garden

E 105 St

2

El Museo del Barrio

53

W 104 St

The Loch

Ravine

E 104 St

20 2

Museum of the City of NY

103 St ❻Ⓒ

C e n t r a l

E 103 St

18 2

NY Academy of Medicine

CENTRAL PARK WEST

W 102 St

P a r k

Girls' Gate

FIFTH AV (Museum Mile)

E 102 St

20 2

22

W 101 St

The Pool

West

E 101 St

20 2

1189

W 100 St

Bridle Path

East Drive

2

1169

W 99 St

North Meadow

Mt Sinai Medical Center

MADISON AV

2

D

W 98 St

North Meadow Security Center

East Meadow

E 98 St

2

2

W 97 St

E 97 St

2

11149 2

96 St ❻Ⓒ

97 St Transverse

2

Woodmen's Gate

E 96 ST

N

Tennis Courts

PAGE 138

PAGE 141

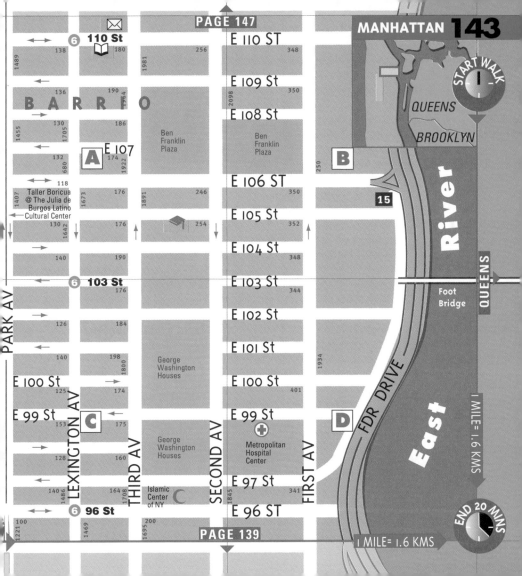

START WALK

QUEENS

BROOKLYN

⊠

6 110 St 📖 180

138

1489

E 110 ST 256 348

E 109 St 350

190 4

1981

136

B A R R I O

190

186

E 108 St

2098

130

1455

1705

Ben Franklin Plaza

Ben Franklin Plaza

186

A E 107

174

132

680

1922

118

1407

176

250

176

1673

1891

246

350

176

130

1642

254

352

140

190

348

6 103 St

176

E 106 ST

15

E 105 St

E 104 St

E 103 St 344

QUEENS

126

184

E 102 St

Foot Bridge

140

198

1800

George Washington Houses

E 101 St

1934

E 100 St

125

174

E 100 St 401

E 99 St

153

C 175

E 99 St

D

128

160

George Washington Houses

Metropolitan Hospital Center

1406

1486

164

1708

Islamic Center of NY

1845

E 97 St 341

6 96 St

E 96 ST

100

1221

1469

1695

200

River

East

River

FDR DRIVE

FIRST AV

SECOND AV

THIRD AV

LEXINGTON AV

PARK AV

Taller Boricua @ The Julia de Burgos Latino Cultural Center

1 MILE= 1.6 KMS

END 20 MINS

1 MILE= 1.6 KMS

PAGE 148

La Salle St

MORNINGSIDE HEIGHTS

Morningside Park Condos

Gen. Grant Houses

Hudson River

RDR West

RDR East

Sakura Park

Manhattan School of Music

Grant's Tomb

Riverside Church

Seminary Rd

Union Theological Seminary

Morningside

Park

A

B

AMSTERDAM AV

Reinhold Niebuhr Pl

W 119 St

Riverside

Park

9A

HENRY HUDSON PKWY

Riverside Dr

Claremont AV

Teachers College

Shapiro Research Center

Butler Hall Terrace

School of International & Public Affairs

Barnard College

Columbia University

St. Pauls Chapel

Buell Hall

Law School

1 9 116 St/Columbia Univ.

Low Mem. Library

C

Butler Library

Women's Hospital

W 114 St

BROADWAY

West End Gate

St Luke's Hospital

W 113 St

D

Cathedral Church of St. John the Divine

W 112 St

Bank St College

W 111 St

Cathedral Pkwy (110 St)

MORNINGSIDE DR

Children's Sculpture Garden

Biblical Garden

1 9

W

PAGE 140

110 ST CATHEDRAL PKWY

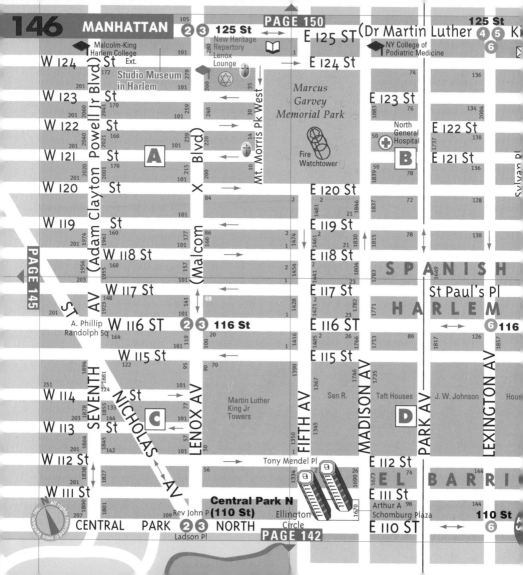

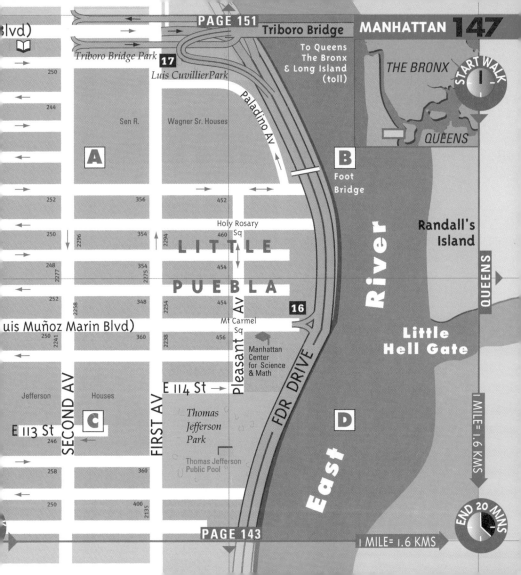

Triboro Bridge

To Queens
The Bronx
& Long Island
(toll)

THE BRONX

START WALK

QUEENS

Blvd)

Triboro Bridge Park **17**

Luis Cuvillier Park

Paladino Av

Sen R.

Wagner Sr. Houses

A

B

Foot
Bridge

Randall's
Island

250

244

252   356   452

250   2296   354   2294   460   Holy Rosary
Sq

L I T T L E

QUEENS

248   2277   354   2275   454

P U E B L A

252   2258   348   2254   454

uis Muñoz Marin Blvd)

250   2241   360   2238   456   Mt Carmel
Sq

16

River

Little
Hell Gate

Pleasant Av

Manhattan
Center
for Science
& Math

Jefferson   Houses

C

E 114 St →

E 113 St
246

SECOND AV

FIRST AV

*Thomas
Jefferson
Park*

D

258   360

250   2135   400

Thomas Jefferson
Public Pool

FDR DRIVE

East

1 MILE= 1.6 KMS

END 20 MINS

1 MILE= 1.6 KMS

START WALK

THE BRONX

QUEENS

PAGE 153

Sugar Shack

W 140 St

W 139 St

West 139th St Playground

W 138 St

Odell M Clark Pl

Abyssinian Baptist

W 137 St

Edgecombe Av

A

W 136 St

Harlem Hospital Center

B

BLVD

Schomburg Ctr

B C 135 St

W 135 ST

135 St **2 3**

E 135 St

DOUGLASS

W 134 St

22 West

Lenox Terrace Pl

W 134 St

Abraham Lincoln Houses

W 133 St

Well's

Lenox Terrace

FREDERICK

(Adam Clayton Powell Jr Blvd)

W 132 St

SEVENTH AV

(Malcom X Blvd)

LENOX AV

E 132 St

W 131 St

E 131 St

FIFTH AV

NICHOLAS

St. Nicholas Houses

E 130 St

MADISON AV

H A R L E M

E 129 St

SAINT

C

E 128 St

D

Harlem State Office Bldg

Langston Hughes Pl

E 127 St

DMV– Traffic Violations

The Black Fashion Museum

Sylvia's

Sydenham NFCC

A W 126 ST

B

125 St BID

Apollo Theater

Alcoholism & Substance Abuse Services

IRS

E 126 St

National Black Theater

C 125 St

W 125 ST

(Dr Martin Luther **2 3** King Jr Blvd)

125 St

D

New Heritage Repertory

PAGE 145

PAGE 150

1 MILE= 1.6 KMS

END 20 MNS

1 MILE= 1.6 KMS

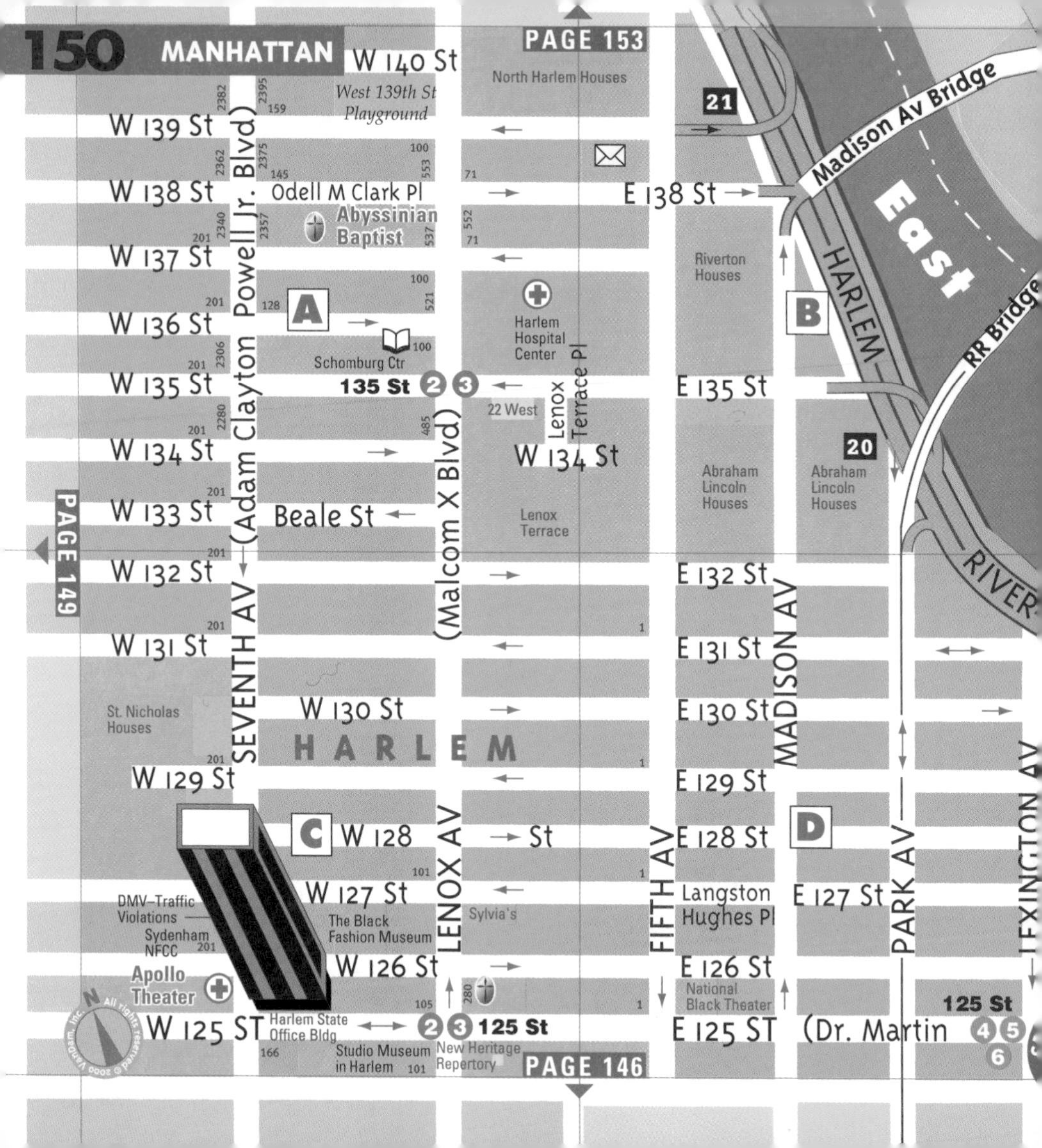

W 140 St

PAGE 153

North Harlem Houses

21

Madison Av Bridge

West 139th St Playground

2382 2395 159

W 139 St

100
2362 2375 145 553

W 138 St   Odell M Clark Pl

E 138 St

2357
2340 201

W 137 St   Abyssinian Baptist

537   552
71

East

HARLEM

Riverton Houses

2306 201
128   100

W 136 St   A

521

B

Schomburg Ctr   100

RR Bridge

2306 201

W 135 St   135 St ② ③

Harlem Hospital Center

E 135 St

2280 201

22 West

W 134 St   485   W 134 St

20

Abraham Lincoln Houses

Abraham Lincoln Houses

201

W 133 St   Beale St

Lenox Terrace

RIVER

201

W 132 St

E 132 St

PAGE 149

201

W 131 St

E 131 St

1

201

W 130 St

E 130 St

St. Nicholas Houses

HARLEM

1

201

W 129 St

E 129 St

C   W 128   St

E 128 St   D

DMV–Traffic Violations Sydenham NFCC   201
101

W 127 St   Sylvia's

Langston Hughes Pl   E 127 St

The Black Fashion Museum

Apollo Theater

W 126 St

National Black Theater

E 126 St

LENOX AV

FIFTH AV

PARK AV

LEXINGTON AV

MADISON AV

SEVENTH AV (Adam Clayton Powell Jr. Blvd)

(Malcom X Blvd)

166
105   280   1

W 125 ST   Harlem State Office Bldg   ② ③ 125 St

E 125 ST   (Dr. Martin   ④ ⑤ ⑥

125 St

Studio Museum in Harlem   101   New Heritage Repertory

PAGE 146

2000 Visitor's

© All rights

THE BRONX
87
E 157 St

THE BRONX

QUEENS

START DRIVE

nial Park Houses

Polo Grounds Houses

Holcombe Rucker Mem. Playground

B

E 151 St

THE BRONX

Macombs Dam Bridge

Harlem

HARLEM RIVER DRIVE

Bronx County

New York County

MAJOR DEEGAN EXPWY

E 150 St

D 155 St

A

271
272
299

300
313

300
307

269

Eugecombe Av

Bradhurst Av

Macombs Pl

295

208
2610

247

210
2574

Frederick Johnson Park

Jackie Robinson Park

255

200
2556

200

2758

3
148 St Lenox Term

Esplanade Gardens Plaza

River

Jackie Robinson Recreation Center

2733

275

2545
2574
2579

200

164
167

167

275

FREDERICK DOUGLASS BLVD

45 St

300

2715

275

2698

320

2643
2690

281

315

2433
2455

200

200
2640

157

161

167

351

SEVENTH AV (Adam Clayton Powell Jr. Blvd)

C

173

2574

145 Street Bridge

145 St 3

Col. C. Young Playground

D

22

15th Infantry Armory NY National Guard

396th Regiment Armory

Chisum Pl

LENOX AV

641

621

Ped Bridge

North Harlem Houses

PAGE 149

THE BRONX

1 MILE= 1.6 KMS

END 3 MINS

1 MILE= 1.6 KMS

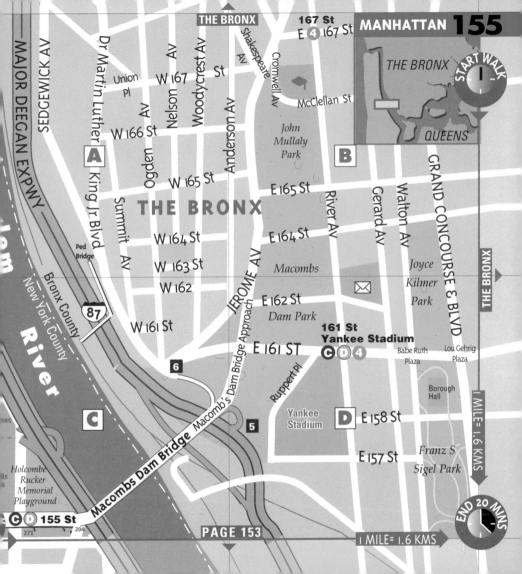

MAJOR DEEGAN EXPWY

SEDGEWICK AV

THE BRONX

167 St
E ④ 167 St

Dr Martin Luther King Jr Blvd

Shakespeare Av

Cromwell Av

THE BRONX

START WALK

Union Pl

Av

W 167 St

W 166 St

Nelson Av

Woodycrest Av

Anderson Av

QUEENS

A

McClellan St

B

John Mullaly Park

Ogden Av

W 165 St

E 165 St

THE BRONX

W 164 St

E 164 St

River Av

Gerard Av

Walton Av

GRAND CONCOURSE & BLVD

THE BRONX

Summit Av

W 163 St

W 162

Macombs

JEROME AV

Joyce Kilmer Park

Ped Bridge

New York County

Bronx County

87

W 161 St

E 162 St

Dam Park

161 St
Yankee Stadium
C D ④

Babe Ruth Plaza

Lou Gehrig Plaza

E 161 ST

1 MILE = 1.6 KMS

6

River

C

5

Macomb's Dam Bridge Approach

Ruppert Pl

Yankee Stadium

D E 158 St

Borough Hall

END 20 MINS

Holcombe Rucker Memorial Playground

Macombs Dam Bridge

E 157 St

Franz S Sigel Park

C D 155 St

271   204

PAGE 153

1 MILE = 1.6 KMS

PAGE 158

Hudson River

A

9A

Gorman
Memorial
Park

Ⓐ **190 St**

W 190 St

Bennett Av

Overlook Ter

BROADWAY

HENRY HUDSON PKWY

RIVERSIDE DRIVE

Chittenden Av

Alex
Rose
Pl

B

W 186 St

WAS

Pinehurst Av

W 185 St

Riverside Dr

Bennett
Park

9

Cabrini

W 183 St

Col. R.
Magaw
Pl

Ⓐ **181 St**

Plaza
Lafayette

Blvd

FT

95

Fort Washington Park

Bus
Terminal

370

700

BROAD

S Pinehurst Av

700

1A

836

353

D

Ⓐ **175**

George Washington **C** Bridge **9** **1** **95**

WASHINGTON AV

Haven

J. Wood
Wright Park

(toll)
To NJ

295

300

126

135 735

277

280 260

W 172 St

715

W 171 St

6

PAGE 154

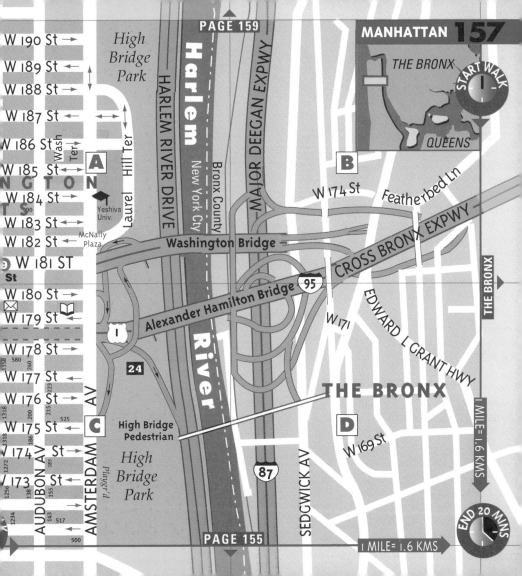

PAGE 160

Inwood Hill Park

Bolton Rd

H. HUDSON PKWY

Payson Av

Beak St

Seaman

Cummin

Dyckman Marina

Dyckman Fields

DYCKMAN

Staff St

Dyckma (200 St)

St

Henshaw St

A

RIVERSIDE DRIVE

B

W. Tigne Triangle

Thaye

17

Playgr'd

Arden

The Cloisters

Margaret

Corbin Dr

Dongan Pl

BROADWAY

Hudson

9A

P

SHERM

9A

Ellwo

16

Fort Tryon Park

Jewish Memorial Hospital

W 196

9

New York County, NY
— · — · — · —
Bergen County, NJ

C

Fort Washington Park

HENRY HUDSON PKWY

Henry Hudson Park

Terrace & Plaza

Promenade

P

D

River

Margaret Corbin Plaza

Bennett Av

BROADWAY

St

Ft Wash

Av

W192

Cabrini Blvd

190 St

W190 St

W190 St

Overlook Ter

PAGE 156

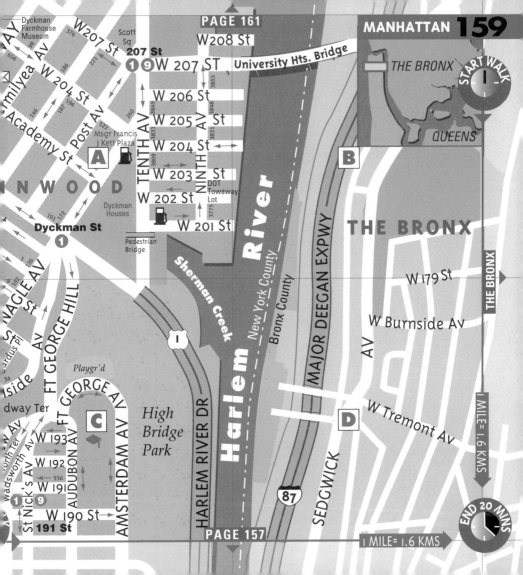

Dyckman Farmhouse Museum

W 207 St

Scott Sq

207 St
❶ ❾ W 207 ST University Hts. Bridge

THE BRONX

START WALK

QUEENS

milyea AV

W 204 St

Academy St

Post Av

Msgr Francis J Kett Plaza

A

TENTH AV

W 206 St

W 205 St

NINTH AV

W 204 St

W 203 St

B

THE BRONX

INWOOD

Dyckman Houses

Dyckman St
❶

W 202 St

DOT Towaway Lot

W 201 St

Pedestrian Bridge

Sherman Creek

New York County

Bronx County

Harlem River

MAJOR DEEGAN EXPWY

W 179 St

W Burnside Av

THE BRONX

NAGLE AV

FT GEORGE HILL

Iside AV

Playgr'd

FT GEORGE AV

C

High Bridge Park

HARLEM RIVER DR

AV

SEDGWICK

W Tremont Av

D

I MILE=1.6 KMS

Broadway Ter

AUDUBON AV

AMSTERDAM AV

W 193 St

W 192 St

W 191 St

wadsworth AV

St Nick's Av

❶ ❾

W 190 St

191 St

87

I MILE= 1.6 KMS

END 20 MINS

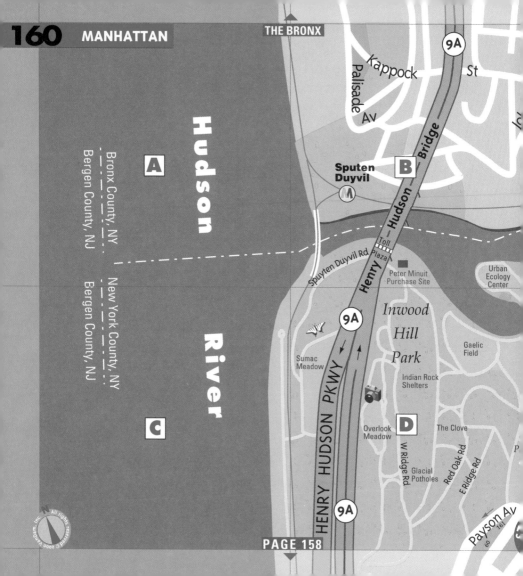

THE BRONX

9A

Kappock St

Palisade Av

Hudson

Sputen Duyvil Ⓜ

B

Hudson Bridge

Bronx County, NY

Bergen County, NJ

A

River

New York County, NY

Bergen County, NJ

C

Toll Plaza

Spuyten Duyvil Rd

Henry

Peter Minuit Purchase Site

Urban Ecology Center

9A

Inwood Hill Park

Gaelic Field

Sumac Meadow

Indian Rock Shelters

HENRY HUDSON PKWY

D

The Clove

Overlook Meadow

W Ridge Rd

Red Oak Rd

E Ridge Rd

Glacial Potholes

9A

Payson Av

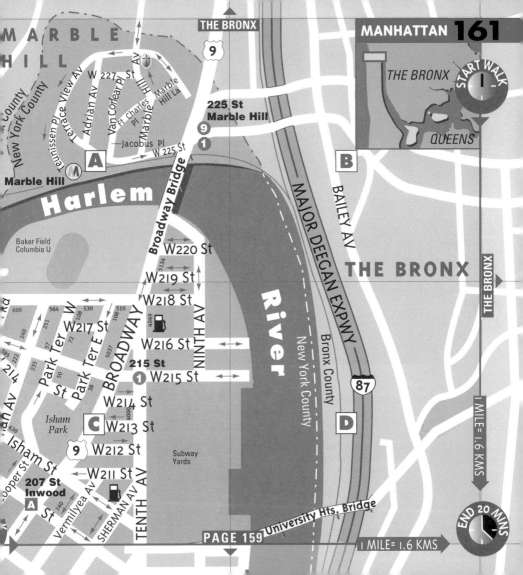

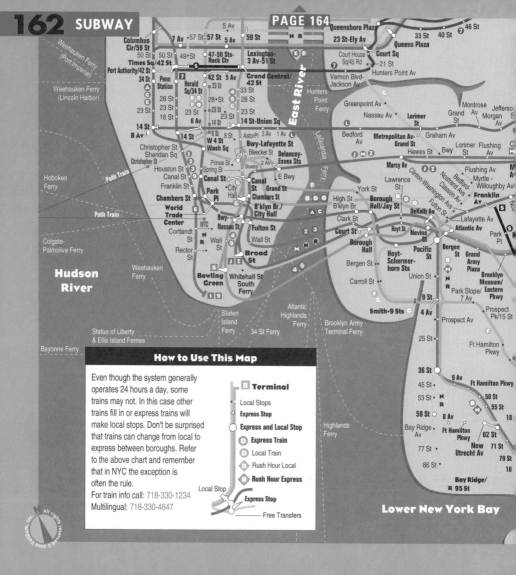

PAGE 164

How to Use This Map

Even though the system generally operates 24 hours a day, some trains may not. In this case other trains fill in or express trains will make local stops. Don't be surprised that trains can change from local to express between boroughs. Refer to the above chart and remember that in NYC the exception is often the rule.

For train info call: 718-330-1234
Multilingual: 718-330-4847

B Terminal

Local Stops

O Express Stop

O Express and Local Stop

P Express Train

D Local Train

B Rush Hour Local

B Rush Hour Express

Free Transfers

Lower New York Bay

QUEENS

MANHATTAN

BROOKLYN

Middle Village/
Metropolitan Av

111 St

104 St

Woodhaven Blvd

85 St-Forest Pkwy

Ozone Park/
Lefferts Blvd

Fresh Pond Rd

Forest Av

75 St

111 St
(Greenwood Av)

Seneca Av

Cypress Hills

104 St (Oxford Av)

Wyckoff Av

Crescent St

Rockaway
Blvd

Halsey St

Norwood Av

88 St

Wilson Av

Bushwick Av-Aberdeen St

Cleveland St

80 St

open 11am-7pm
racing days

Grant Av

Shuttle Bus-
Q3, Q10, B15

s Halsey
St

Bwy-
Eastern Pkwy

Van Siclen Av

Euclid
Av

Aqueduct
Racetrack

Aqueduct/
N. Conduit
Av

JFK
Airport

Chauncey St

Alabama Av

Shepherd Av

Rock-
away
Av

Bwy-
East New
York

Atlantic Av

Liberty
Av

Van Siclen Av

Howard Beach
JFK Airport

Sutter Av

Van Siclen
Av

Crown Hts/
Utica Av

Rockaway
Av

New Lots Av

Sutter Av
Rutland Rd

Saratoga
Av

Junius
St

Pennsylvania Av

Livonia Av

New Lots Av

resident St

E 105 St

Sterling St

Winthrop St

Canarsie/
Rockaway Pkwy

Church Av

Beverly Rd

**Jamaica
Bay**

Newkirk Av

verly Rd

Cortelyou Rd

Newkirk Av

Brooklyn
College/
Flatbush Av

Av H

Av J

Broad Channel

Av M

BROOKLYN

Far Rockaway/
Mott Av

Pkwy

Kings Hwy

Beach 25 St

N

Beach 36 St

Av P

Kings Hwy

Av U

Beach 44 St

Neck Rd

Beach 90 St

Beach 60 St

Av U

Sheepshead
Bay

Beach 98 St

Beach
67 St

Av X

Av U

Beach 105 St

86 St

Neptune
Av

Brighton Beach

50 St

Ocean Pkwy

Rockaway Park
Beach 116 St

Atlantic Ocean

y Island/
illwell Av

NY Aquarium/W 8 St

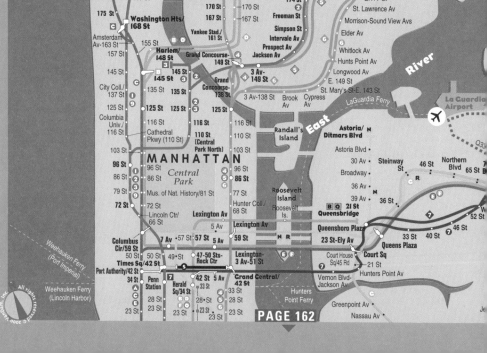

THE
BRONX

MANHATTAN

Central Park

Van Cortlandt Pk/242 St
242 St
238 St
231 St
Marble Hill/225 St
207 St
Dyckman St
190 St
181 St
175 St
Washington Hts/168 St
Amsterdam Av-163 St
157 St
155 St
145 St
City Coll./137 St
135 St
125 St
Columbia Univ./116 St
116 St
Cathedral Pkwy (110 St)
103 St
96 St
86 St
79 St
72 St
Lincoln Ctr/66 St
Columbus Cir/59 St
50 St
Port Authority/42 St
Times Sq/42 St
34 St
Penn Station
28 St
23 St

Dyckman St
207 St
191 St
181 St
Harlem/148 St
145 St
145 St
135 St
125 St
116 St
110 St
103 St
96 St
86 St
77 St
Mus. of Nat. History/81 St
72 St
Lexington Av
5 Av
57 St
50 St
49 St
47-50 Sts-Rock Ctr
42 St
5 Av
33 St
28 St
23 St

Mosholu Pkwy
Lehman College/Bedford Pk Blvd
Kingsbridge Rd
Fordham Rd
183 St
Burnside Av
176 St
Mt Eden Av
170 St
167 St
Yankee Stad./161 St
Grand Concourse-149 St
Grand Concourse-138 St

205 St Norwood
Bedford Park Blvd
Kingsbridge Rd
Fordham Rd
182-183 St
Tremont Av
174-175 St
170 St
167 St
Freeman St
Simpson St
Intervale Av
Prospect Av
Jackson Av
3 Av-149 St
3 Av-138 St
Brook Av
Cypress Av

Woodlawn
233 St
225 St
219 St
Gun Hill Rd
Burke Av
Allerton Av
Pelham Pkwy
Bronx Park East
E. 180 St
W. Farms Sq-E. Tremont Av
174 St
St. Lawrence Av
Morrison-Sound View Avs
Elder Av
Whitlock Av
Hunts Point Av
Longwood Av
E. 149 St
St. Mary's St-E. 143 St

Wakefield/241 St
Nereid Av
Eastchester/Dyre Av
Baychester Av
Pelham Bay Park
Gun Hill Rd
Pelham Pkwy
Morris Pk
Buhre Av
Middletown Rd
Westchester Sq-E. Tremont Av
Zerega Av
Castle Hill Av
Parkchester/E.177 St

Randall's Island
Roosevelt Island
Roosevelt Is.
Hunter Coll./68 St
Lexington Av
59 St
5 Av
Lexington-3 Av-51 St
Grand Central/42 St
Herald Sq/34 St
5 Av
33 St

East River
LaGuardia Ferry
La Guardia Airport

Astoria/Ditmars Blvd
Astoria Blvd
30 Av
Broadway
36 Av
39 Av
21 St
Queensbridge
Queensboro Plaza
23 St-Ely Av
Court House Sq/45 Rd
Court Sq
21 St
Hunters Point Av
Vernon Blvd-Jackson Av
Greenpoint Av
Nassau Av

Steinway St
46 St
Northern Blvd
65 St
36 St
33 St
40 St
46 St
52 St

Hunters Point Ferry

Weehauken Ferry (Port Imperial)
Weehauken Ferry (Lincoln Harbor)

PAGE 162

Express Trains	Local Trains	Rush Hour Trains

Here's how New Yorkers used to refer to the lines of their system

Express Trains	Local Trains	Rush Hour Trains
② ③ ④ ⑤	① ⑨ Skip-Stop Service in Upper Manhattan during rush hour ⑥ ⑦	◆ Brooklyn & The Bronx
Ⓐ Ⓔ Queens	Ⓐ Brooklyn after 9 pm & weekends Ⓒ Ⓔ Manhattan Ⓢ	◆ Rockaway
Ⓑ Manhattan & Bklyn eves	Ⓑ Brooklyn 36 St–Coney Island late nights Ⓒ	◆ Manhattan 59 St - Bklyn 36 St
Ⓓ Manhattan	Ⓓ Brooklyn & The Bronx	◆ Manhattan 59 St - 168 St
Ⓙ Ⓩ Queens Myrtle-Marcy Av, Manhattan	Ⓕ Manhattan & Brooklyn	◆ Manh & Bronx ◇ Bklyn
	Ⓙ evenings Ⓜ	◆ Queens 71 Av - Queens Plaza
Ⓚ No service after 9pm. Queens use B train, Brooklyn use D train.	Ⓝ Ⓡ	Ⓝ Brooklyn
	Ⓢ Shuttle	Ⓝ Queens & Manhattan
	Ⓛ Canarsie	

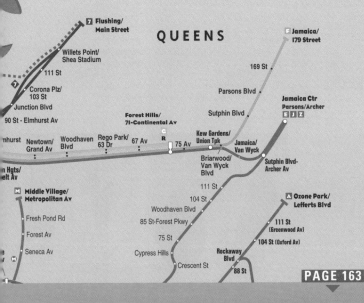

THE BRONX

QUEENS

MANHATTAN

QUEENS

⑦ Flushing/Main Street

Ⓕ Jamaica/179 Street

Willets Point/Shea Stadium

169 St

111 St

Corona Plz/103 St

Parsons Blvd

Junction Blvd

Sutphin Blvd

Jamaica Ctr Parsons/Archer Ⓔ Ⓙ Ⓩ

90 St - Elmhurst Av

Forest Hills/71-Continental Av

Kew Gardens/Union Tpk

Newtown/Grand Av

Woodhaven Blvd

Rego Park/63 Dr

67 Av

Ⓡ

75 Av

Jamaica/Van Wyck

Sutphin Blvd-Archer Av

n Hgts/elt Av

Briarwood/Van Wyck Blvd

Ⓜ Middle Village/Metropolitan Av

111 St

Ⓐ Ozone Park/Lefferts Blvd

Fresh Pond Rd

104 St

Woodhaven Blvd

Forest Av

85 St-Forest Pkwy

111 St (Greenwood Av)

Seneca Av

75 St

104 St (Oxford Av)

Cypress Hills

Rockaway Blvd

Crescent St

88 St

PAGE 163

200 NEIGHBORHOODS

Page
Grid

Alphabet City ..114D
Battery Park City ....
..................102A
Carnegie Hill ..138B
Chelsea 117A
Chinatown 107C
Civic Center 104B
Clinton 124B
Diamond District ....
..................125D
DoMa 102B
East Midtown..122B
East Village 114B
El Barrio 146D
Flatiron 117D
Flower Market ....
..................117A
Fashion District ......
..................117A
Garment District ....
..................121A
Gold Coast 130D
Gramercy Park ......
..................118D
Greenwich Village..
..................113D
Hamilton Hts ..152D
Harlem............149C
Inwood 159A
Kips Bay 123C
Koreatown 121D
Lincoln Sq......128D
Little India......118B
Little Italy 107A
Little Puebla....147A
LoHO 110B
Lower East Side......
..................107D
Manhattanville ....
..................148B
Marble Hill 161A
Meatmarket 112A
Midtown East..126D
Morningside Hts ....
..................144B
Murray Hill 122D
NoHo 110A

Nolita................107A
Rockefeller Center
..................125B
S SoHo 106B
SoHo 106B
S Village 109A
Spanish Harlem ......
..................146B
Stuyvesant Town ....
..................119C
Theater District ......
..................125C
TriBeCa 104A
Turtle Bay 127A
Two Bridges 107C
Union Square ....
..................118D
Upper West Side ....
..................132B-140D
Washington Hts......
..................156B
Wechee 116D
West Village ...112B
World Financial
Center (WFC)..104C
World Trade Center
(WTC) 104D
Yorkville........139D

TO FIND A BASIC

Simply turn to
page and locate
the basic in
grids A,B,C or D.

AIRPORTS & HELIPORTS
Floyd Bennet Field (CAN), BK 439C
LaGuardia (LGA), QS 2
JFK International (JFK), QS 2
Newark International (EWR) NJ 2
Teterboro (TEB), NJ............................2
Wall St Heliport, MA 103C
30 St Heliport, MA..........................120C
34 St Heliport, MA..........................123D
60 St Heliport, MA..........................131D

BUS & TRAIN TERMINALS
George Washington Br, MA................156D
Grand Central Station, MA 122B
Penn Station, MA 121C
Port Authority, MA 121A
PATH WTC, MA 104D

FERRY TERMINALS
Governor's Island 103C
Liberty & Ellis Island.......................102D
South St Seaport, Pier 17 ....103B
South Ferry 103A
Staten Island 103C
Wall St, Pier 11 ....103B
Whitehall, Slip 5..............................103C
World Financial Center 104C
Yankee Stadium (The Bronx) 155D
E 34 St 123C
E 90 St 139D
W 38 St, Pier 78 ....120A

TUNNELS & BRIDGES
Alexander Hamilton Br 1
Bayonne Br (toll) ....
Broadway Br..1
Bronx-Whitestone Br (toll) ....
Brooklyn Battery Tun (toll) 1
Brooklyn Br 1
Cross Bay Mem (toll)............................
George Washington Br (toll)..................1
Goethals Br (toll)...................................
Henry Hudson Br (toll)...........................1
Holland Tun (toll) 1
Lincoln Tun (toll)...................................1
Macombs Dam Br 1
Madison Av Br 1
Manhattan Br 1
Queens Midtown Tun (toll) 1
Queensboro Br 1
Roosevelt Island Br 3
Throgs Neck Br (toll) 1
Triboro Br (toll) 1
University Hts Br 1
Verrazano Narrows Br (toll) ....
Washington Br 1
Whitestone Br (toll) ....
Williamsburg Br 1
Willis Av Br 1
3 Av Br 1

THINK
UNFOLDS

MANHATTAN

A Phillip Randolph
.................145C
Abingdon Sq ...112B
Abraham A. Kazan
St 111A
Adam Clayton
Powell Jr Bd ....
.............145A-153A
Adrian Av 161A
Albany St 102B
Alex Rose Pl...156B
Alexander
Hamilton Sq ...152B
Allen St...........107B
Amsterdam Av ....
.........128D-159C
Ann St 105C
Academy St 159A
Archbishop F J
Green Pl 122B
Green St 158B
Asser Levy Pl..119A
Astor Pl 113B
Attorney St......111A
Audubon ....
...........154B-159C
Audubon Ter ..152B
Av A-B 114D
Av C 115C
Av D 115C
Av of The Americas
...........106B-129D
Av of the Finest .....
.........................105A
Battery Pk City
Broadway Ter 158D
Battery Pk St 112C
Bankers Trust Plz...
.........................104D
Barclay St 104D
Barrow St 108B
Baruch Dr.......111A
Baruch Pl 111B
Battery Pl 102B
Baxter St 105A
Bayard St 107C
Beach St.........106C

Beak St 158B
Beaver St 102A
Bedford St 109A
Beekman Pl 127A
Beekman St 105C
Bennett Av 156B
Benson Pl.......105A
Bethune St 112B
Bleecker St 109A
Bloomfield St ..112A
Bogardus Pl ...159C
Bond St 113D
Bowery 107A
Bradhurst Av 153A
Bridge St 102D
Broad St 103A
Broadway ....
.................102B-161B
Broadway Al ...118B
Broadway Ter 158D
Broome St 106A
Cabrini Bd 156B
Canal St 106A-110D
Cannon St.......111A
Carder Rd
(Governors Is) 406C
Cardinal Hayes Pl ..
.........................105A
Cardinal Stepinac
Pl 120B
Carlisle St.......102B
Carmine St 109A
Cathedral Pkwy 140A
Catherine La ...105A
Catherine Slip 105B
Catherine St...105C
Cedar St 102C
Central Park N141A
Central Park S 129C
Central Park W.......
.............129A-142A
Centre Market Pl ....
.........................107A
Centre St105A-110C
Chambers St ..104A
Charles La 112D
Charles St.......112D
Charlton St.....109A

Chase Manhattan
Plz 103A
Chatham Sq ...105B
Cherokee Pl ...135D
Cherry St 105B
Chisum St 153D
Chittenden Av 156B
Christopher St 108B
Chrystie St 107A
Church St........104B
Claremont Av ..144A
Clarkson St....108B
Cleveland Pl...109D
Cliff St 105C
Clinton St 110B
Coenties Al.....103A
Coenties Slip .103A
Col R Magaw Pl .....
.........................156B
Collister St......106A
Columbia St ...111A
Columbus Av ....
.............128D-140D
Columbus Cir .129C
Commerce St..108B
Convent Av.....148D
Convent Hill ...148D
Cooper Sq......114C
Cooper St 158B
Cornelia St.....113C
Cortlandt Al ...106D
Cortlandt St ...104D
Craig Rd N & S
(Governors Is) 406C
Crosby St 105B
Cumming St ...158B
Dag Hammarskjold
Plz 127C
Delancey St ...110D
Depew Pl 126B
Desbrosses St 106A
Dey St 104D
Division Rd
(Governors Is) 406C
Division St 105B
Dr Martin Luther
King Jr Bd...............
.............146B-151C

Dominick St 106A
Donellon Sq ...152B
Dongan Pl.......158B
Douglass Cir ..141A
Douglass St ...105D
Dover St 105D
Downing St 109A
Doyers St 105A
Duane St.........104B
Duarte Sq 109C
Duffy Sq 125C
Duke Ellington Bd ..
.........................140A
Duke Ellington Cir ..
.........................142B
Dutch St 105C
Dyckman St ...158B
Dyer Av 120D
Early Bird Rd
(Governors Is) 406C
East Dr
(Roosevelt Is)..308C
East Dr ..130B-142A
E Broadway ....
.............105B-111C
East End Av ...135B
E Houston St ..114C
Edgar Allan Poe St
.........................132B
Edgar St 102B
Edgecombe Av149A
Edward M Morgan
Pl 152B
Eldridge St 107B
Elizabeth St ...107A
Elk St 105A
Ellwood St 158D
Enright Rd
(Governors Is) 406C
Ericsson Pl 106A
Essex St 110B
Exchange Al....102B
Exchange Pl...102B
Exterior St 159B
Extra Pl 110A
Fairview Av 159C
Fashion Av 117A
Father Demo Sq .....
.........................113C

Father Fagan Sq. ....
.........................109A
FDR Dr .. 103C-151C
Finn Sq 104B
Fletcher St 103A
Foley Sq 105A
Forsyth St 107B
Ft Charles Pl...161A
Ft George Av ..159C
Ft George Hill .159C
Ft Washington Av ..
.........................154C
Frankfort St ...105C
Franklin Pl 106D
Franklin St 104B
Federal Plz 105A
Frederick Douglass
Bd 145C-153C
Freedom Pl......128A
Freeman Al.....110A
Front St 103A
Ft George Av ..159C
Ft Washington Av ..
.........................158D
Fulton St 104D
Galvin Av 120B
Gansevoort St 112A
Gateway Plz...102A
Gay St 113A
Gold St 103A
Gouverneur La 103A
Gouverneur St 111C
Gouverneur Slip
W & E 111C
Gracie Sq 139D
Gracie Ter 135B
Gramercy Park
N & S 118D
Grand Army Plz129D
Grand St 106B
Great Jones St113D
Greeley Sq 121D
Greene St 106B
Greenwich Av 112B
Greenwich St ....
.............102B-112B
Gresham Rd
(Governors Is) 406C

Grove Ct 112D
Grove St 112D
Gulf Western Plz ....
.........................129C
H Howard Sq ..107A
Hamill Pl 105A
Hamilton Pl....148B
Hamilton Ter ..152D
Hancock Pl.....144B
Hancock Sq ...145A
Hanover Sq 103A
Hanover St 103A
Harlem River Dr .....
.............153A-159C
Harrison St.....104A
Haven Av 154A
Hay Rd
(Governors Is) 406C
Henderson Pl..135B
Henry Hudson Pkwy
(9A) 128C-160D
Henry J Browne
Bd 136D
Henry St 105B
Henshaw St ...158B
Herald Sq 121D
Hester St 107A
Hillside Av 159C
Hogan Pl.........105A
Holy Rosary Sq147B
Horatio St.......112A
Howard St 106B
Hubert St 106C
Hudson Sq 106A
Hudson St ....
.............104B-112B
Independence Plz ..
.........................104A
Indian Rd 161C
Irving Pl 118D
Isham St 161C
J.P. Ward St ...102B
Jackson Sq 112B
Jackson St......111D
Jacobus Pl 161A
James St.........107C
James Madison Plz
.........................105B

Jane St 112A
Jay St 104B
Jefferson St.....107B
Jersey St 109B
John St 103A
Jones Al 110A
Jones St 113C
Jumel Ter 154D
Jumel Pl 154B
Kenmare St 107A
Kimlau Sq 105A
King St 109A
La Salle St 144B
Lafayette St ....
............105A-114C
Lafayette Ct ...113B
La Guardia Pl..109B
Laight St 106A
Langston Hughes
Pl 149D
Laurel Hill Ter 157A
Legion Mem Sq103A
Lenox Av145D-153D
Lenox Ter 149B
Leonard St 104B
Leroy St 108B
Lewis St 111B
Lexington Av...........
...............118B-150D
Liberty Pl 104D
Liberty St 102B
Lincoln Sq 128B
Lincoln Plz 128D
Lincoln Tunnel
Entrance.........120D
Lispenard St...106B
Little West St..102B
Little W 12 St ..112A
Louise Nevelson
Plz 103A
Ludlow St 107B
Luis Muñoz Marin
Bd 147C
MacDougal Al 113A
MacDougal St 109A
Macombs Pl...153A
Madison Av ....
............118A-150B

Madison Sq Plz ......
...........................118A
Madison Sq N 118A
Madison St.....105B
Maher Cir 153A
Maiden La 103A
Main St (Roosevelt
Island)...........308A
Mangin St.......111B
Malcom X Bd ....
............145D-153D
Manhattan Av ....
............145D-153D
Marble Hill Av 161A
Marble Hill La 161A
Margaret Corbin Dr
........................158B
Margaret Corbin
Plz 158D
Market Slip 107D
Market St 107D
Marketfield St 103A
McCarthy Sq ..113A
McKenna Sq ..154B
McNally Plz 157A
Mercer St.......106B
Mill La 103A
Milligan Pl 113A
Minetta La 113C
Minetta St 109A
Mitchell Pl 127C
Mitchell Sq 154B
Monroe St 105B
Mott St ..105A-114C
Msgr Francis J
Kett Plz 159A
Montefiore Sq 148B
Montgomery St111C
Moore St........103C
Morningside Av144B
Morningside Dr 144D
Morris St 102B
Morton St.......108B
Mosco St 105A
Mott St 105A
Mt Carmel Sq.145D
Mt Morris Pk W ......
........................145B

Mulberry St 105A
Murray St 104C
Museum Mile ....
...........133B-142B
N D Perlman Pl ......
........................119C
Nagle Av 159C
Nassau St.......103A
New St 102B
Norfolk St.......110B
N Moore St 104A
North End Av ..104C
Odell M Clark Pl .....
........................149A
Old B'way 148D
Old Slip 103A
Oliver St 105B
Orchard St 107B
Overlook Ter ..156B
Paladino Av ...147B
Park Av..122D-150D
Park Av South 118D
Park Pl 104D
Park Pl W 104A
Park Row 105C
Park Ter E & W ....
........................161C
Patchin Pl......113A
Payson Av 158B
Pearl St..........102D
Peck Slip 105D
Pell St 105A
Penn Plz 121C
Peretz Sq 110B
Perry St..........112D
Pershing Sq....122B
Peter Cooper Rd ....
........................119A
Peter Minuit Plz .....
........................103C
Pike Slip 107D
Pike St...........105A
Pine St 108B
Pinehurst Av ..156B
Pitt St 111A
Platt St 103A
Plz Lafayette ..156D
Pleasant Av 147D

Police Plz 105A
Pomander Wk 136B
Post Av 159A
Prince St........109A
Printing House Sq ..
........................105C
Queens Midtown
Tunnel Entrance......
........................122D
Reade St........104B
Rector Pl.........102A
Rector St 102B
Reinhold Niebuhr
Pl 144A
Renwick St......106A
Rev P Ladson Pl.....
........................146C
Ridge St 111A
River Rd (Roosevelt
Island)...........308A
River Ter 104C
Riverside Drive .....
...........132C-158B
Riverside Dr E & W
........................144A
Riverside Dr ....
........................148C
Viaduct 148C
Riverview Ter..131D
Rivington St ...110B
Robert F. Wagner
Sr. Pl 105B
Rockefeller Plz 125D
Roosevelt Sq ..148D
Rose St 105A
Rutgers St 107D
Rutherford Pl..118D
Ryders Al 105C
St Clair Pl 148C
St James Pl ...105A
St Johns La 106B
St Josephs La 106A
St Lukes Pl.....108B
St Mark's Pl ...114A
St Pauls Pl 146D
St Nicholas Av ....
...........145A-157C
St Nicholas Pl 153A
St Nicholas Ter 149C

Samuel Dickstein
Plz 111C
Schiff Pkwy 110D
Scott Sq 159A
Seaman Av 156B
Seminary Rd ..144B
Sheridan Sq ...113C
Sheriff St........115C
Sherman Av ...158B
Sherman St ...128B
Sheriff St 111A
Shinbone Al ...113D
Shona Bailey Pl ....
........................148B
Sickles St 158B
Sniffen Ct 122D
South End Av ..102A
South St 103A-111B
S Pinhurst Av..156D
S William St ...103A
Spring St.........106A
Spruce St 105C
Stable Ct 113D
Staff St 158B
Stanton St 110B
Staple St.........104B
State St 102D
Stone St 103C
Straus Sq 107B
Stuyvesant Al 114A
Stuyvesant Sq 119C
Stuyvesant St 114A
Suffolk St 110B
Sullivan St 109A
Sutton Pl 131D
Sutton Pl S 127A
Sutton Sq 131D
Sylvan Pl........146B
Sylvan Ter 154D
Szold Pl..........115A
Taras Shevchenko
Pl 114C
Terrace View Av ....
........................161A
Teunissen Pl ..161A
Thames St 102B
Thayer St 158B
Theater Row ..120B

Theatre Al 1
Thomas St 1
Thompson St ..1
Times Sq 1
Tiemann Pl 1
Tompkins Sq....1
Trans Manhattan
Expwy 19
Trimble Pl 1
Trinity Pl 1
Trump Plz 1
Tudor City Pl...1:
Tunnel Entrance
........................1:
Tunnel Exit St..1:
Union Sq E & N ...
Union Sq W 1
University Pl....1
University Plz..1
Van Corlear Pl 16
Vandam St 1
Vanderbilt Av ..1:
Varick St 1
Vermilyea Av ..1!
Verdi Sq 1:
Vesey St 1
Vestry St 1
Village Sq 1
W Houston St 1
W C Handy Pl 1
W Tigne Triangle
........................1:
W Union Plz 1
Wadsworth Av1!
Wadsworth Ter 1!
Walker St 1
Wall St 1
Wanamaker Pl1
Warren St........1
Wash Pl 1
Washington Sq
E & N...............1
Washington Sq
S & W 1
Washington Mew
........................1
Washington Sq1

shington St	9 Av 116D-124B,161C	E 118-25 St 146B
........102B-112B	10 Av	E 126-32 St 150D
shington Ter157A	......116D-124B,161C	E 135 St 150B
ter St 103A	11 Av 116B-124B	E 138 St 150B
tts St 106A	12 Av	W 3 St 113C
verly Pl 112B	......116A-124B,148C	W 4 St 112B
ehawken St108A	65 St Transverse	W 8-9 St 113A
Broadway ..104B	........................130A	W 10-11 St 112D
est End Av	79 St Transverse	W 12-14 St 112A
........128C-140A	........................133A	W 15-21 St 116D
Houston St 108B	85 St Transverse	W 22-25 St 116B
est Side Hwy	........................137C	W 26-29 St 116A
........102C-124A	97 St Transverse	W 30-36 St 120B
est Dr..129C-141A	........................137A	W 37-38 St 120B
est Rd		W 39-44 St 120A
osevelt Is)..308A	E 1-2 St 110A	W 45-49 St 124D
est St 102B	E 3 St 114C	W 50-57 St 124D
Thames St..102A	E 4 St 113D	W 58-64 St 128D
Washington Pl...	E 5-6 St 114C	W 65-72 St 128D
........................113C	E 7 St 114A	W 73-79 St 132C
heeler Rd	E 8 St 113B	W 80-86 St 132A
overnors Is) 406C	E 9-14 St 113B	W 87-91 St 136C
hite St 106B	E 15-20 St 117D	W 92-99 St 136A
hitehall St......103C	E 21 St 118A	W 100-03 St 140D
llett St..........111C	E 22-29 St 118A	W 104-09 St 140A
lliam St..........103A	E 30-36 St 121D	W 111-17 St 145C
ooster St........106B	E 37-40 St 121B	W 118-25 St 145A
orth Sq 117B	E 41-43 St 122A	W 126-29 St 148D
orth St 104B	E 44-49 St 125D	W 130-32 St 148C
rk Av ..131D-139D	E 50 St 125B	W 133 St 148C
rk St..............106B	E 51 St 126B	W 134 St 148B
	E 52-57 St 126A	W 135-40 St 148A
MBERED	E 58-64 St 130D	W 141-49 St 152D
• Pl • ST	E 65-72 St 130B	W 150-59 St 152B
Av 110B-147A	E 73-79 St 133D	W 160-64 St 154D
Pl..................102D	E 80-82 St 133B	W 165-68 St 154B
Av 110A-151C	E 83-86 St 134B	W 169-73 St 154A
Pl..................102B	E 87-91 St 137D	W 174-80 St 157C
Av 114C-150D	E 92-95 St 137B	W 181-90 St 157A
Pl..................102B	E 96-99 St 138B	W 191-93 St 159C
Av 113B	E 100 St 143C	W 196 St 158D
Av 113B-150B	E 101-03 St 141D	W 201-07 St 159A
Av 106B-129D	E 104-07 St 141B	W 208 St 159A
Av 117C-130C	E 108-10 St 142B	W 211-18 St 161C
........145C-153A	E 111-12 St 146D	W 219-20 St 161A
Av S 109A	E 113-14 St 147C	W 225 St 161A
Av 112B-125A	E 115-17 St 146D	W 227 St 161A

Arithmetic of The Avenues

To locate an address on an avenue in Manhattan without knowing the cross street is quite simple. Just drop the last figure, divide by 2 and add or subtract as listed below. The resulting number is the nearest cross street. This does not apply to Broadway below 8 St.

Avs A, B, C, D add 3	**Broadway**
1 & 2 Av add 3	754–858 subtract 29
3 Av add 10	858–958 subtract 25
4 Av add 8	> 100 St subtract 30
5 Av to 200 add 13	**Columbus Av** add 60
to 400 add 16	**Convent Av** add 127
to 600 add 18	**Central Park W** divide St
to 775 add 20	number by 10 & add 60
to 1500 add 45	**Edgecombe Av** add 134
to 2000 add 24	**Lenox Av** add 110
to 775 - 1286 drop last	**Lexington Av** add 22
figure & subtract 18	**Madison Av** add 26
to 1500 add 45	**Manhattan Av** add 100
to 2000 add 24	**Park Av** add 35
Av of the Americas subtract 12	**Pleasant Av** add 101
7 Av add 12, > 110 St add 20	**Riverside Dr** divide house
8 Av add 10	number by 10 & add 72
9 Av add 13	up to 165 St
10 Av add 14	**West End Av** add 60
Amsterdam Av add 60	
Audubon Av add 165	

East	Cross Streets	West

To find a crosstown street address and
the avenues it is in between, follow the key.

Manhattanwide	**Below 59th St**	**Above 59th Street**
1–49 5–Madison Avs	**1–99** 5–6 Avs	**1–99** Central Park W–Columbus Avs
50–99 Madison–Park Avs	**100–199** 6–7 Avs	**100–199** Columbus–Amsterdam Avs
100–149 Park–Lexington Avs	**200–299** 7–8 Avs	**200–299** Amsterdam–West End Avs (WEA)
149–199 Lex–3 Avs	**300–399** 8–9 Avs	**300–399** West End Av–Riverside Dr
200–299 3–2 Avs	**400–499** 9–10 Avs	
300–399 2–1 Avs	**500–599** 10–11 Avs	
400–499 1–York Avs (Av A below 14 St)		
500–599 Avs A–B		

EMERGENCIES

AAA Road Service
800-222-4357

Ambulance, Fire, Police 911

Animal Medical Center
212-838-8100

Arson Hotline
718-722-3600

Battered Women
800-621-4673

Coast Guard
800-735-3415

Child Abuse
800-342-3720

Dental Emergency
212-677-2510

Domestic Violence
800-621-4673

Drug Abuse
800-395-3400

Emergency Medical Technician Info
718-416-7000

Hazardous Materials (EPA)
718-699-9811

Locksmith (24hr)
212-247-6747

Missing Persons
212-719-9000

Park Emergencies
(24hr) 800-201-7275

Pharmacy (24hr)
212-989-3632

Poison Control Center (24hr)
212-764-7667

Rape Hotline
212-577-7777

Runaway Hotline
212-966-8000

Sex Crimes Reports
212-267-7273

Suicide Prevention
212-532-2400

Victim Services Hotline
212-577-7777

ESSENTIALS

AAA
212-757-2000

B & B Reservations
212-737-7049

Bridge & Tunnels
212-221-9903

ChequePoint USA
212-869-6281

Convention & Visitor's Bureau
212-397-8222

Customs (24hr)
800-697-3662

Directory Assistance 411

Foreign Exchange Rates
212-883-0400

Immigration
212-264-5650

Hotel Reservations
800-444-7666

Jacob Javits Convention Center
212-216-2000

Lost Travelers Checks
• AMEX
800-221-7282
• Citicorp
800-645-6556
• VISA
800-227-6811

Movies
212-777-FILM

NYC On Stage
212-768-1818

Passport Info
212-399-5290

Post Office
212-967-8585

Telegrams
800-325-6000

Time
212-976-1616

Traffic Information
212-442-7080

Traveler's Aid
212-577-7700

UN Information
212-963-1234

Wake-Up Call
212-540-9000

Weather
212-976-1212

TOURS & EXCURSIONS

Adventure on a Shoestring
212-265-2633

All American Stage Tours
800-735-8530

Art Tours
212-239-4160

Backstage at Broadway
212-575-8065

Big Apple Greeters
212-669-2896

Big Onion Tours
212-439-1090

Bronx Heritage Trail 718-881-8900

Brooklyn Historical Society
718-624-0890

City Walks
212-989-2456

Circle Line
212-563-3200

Doorways to Design
718-339-1542

Ellis Island Ferry
212-269-5755

Gray Line NY Tours
212-397-2600

Harlem Renaissance
212-722-9534

Harlem CVB
212-427-33

Hoboken Ferry (NJ)
201-420-4422

Liberty Helicopters
212-967-6464

Manhattan Sightseeing
212-354-5122

Municipal Arts Society
212-980-1297

NY Big Apple Tours Double Decker Tours
212-967-6008
212-691-7866

NY Helicopter
800-645-3494

NY Waterway
800-53-FERRY

Parents League of NY 212-737-7385

The Petrel (1938)
212-825-1976

The Pioneer (1885)
212-669-9417

Radical Tours
718-462-0069

Seaport Music Cruises
212-630-8888

Seastreak
800-262-8743

Spirit Cruises
212-727-2789

Urban Explorations
718-721-5254

Walking Tours of Chinatown
212-619-4785

Wild Food & Ecology Tours
718-291-6825

World Yacht Cruises
212-630-8100

92nd St. YM–YWHA
212-996-1100

TRANSPORT

Airlines–Domestic
• American
800-433-7300
• Continental
800-523-3273
• Delta
800-221-1212
• Northwest
800-441-1818
• TWA
800-221-2000
• United
800-241-6522
• USAir
800-428-4322

Airlines–Foreign
• Aeromexico
800-237-6639
• Air Canada
800-776-3000
• Air France
800-321-4538
• ANA–ALL Nippon
800-235-9262
• British Airways
800-247-9297
• Lufthansa
800-645-3880

Then.

**ConEd
Billing**

**ConEd
Repairs**

**ConEd
Installation**

**ConEd
Bronx**

**ConEd
Steam**

**ConEd
Gas**

**ConEd
Maintenance**

**ConEd
Westchester**

**ConEd
Electric**

**ConEd
Brooklyn**

**ConEd
Staten Island**

**ConEd
Safety**

**ConEd
Distribution**

**ConEd
Manhattan**

**ConEd
Queens**

Now.

ConEd Direct

Introducing ConEd Direct. In a world gone mad with phone numbers, Con Edison announces just one convenient, toll-free number. One number to reach all of Con Edison's customer service departments, 1-800-75-CONED. It's easy to remember, too. Call 1-800-75-CONED for your customer service needs 24 hours a day, 7 days a week.

Con Edison
The Company You Know.
The People You Trust.

1-800-75-CONED

Now One Call Solves It All.

www.coned.com

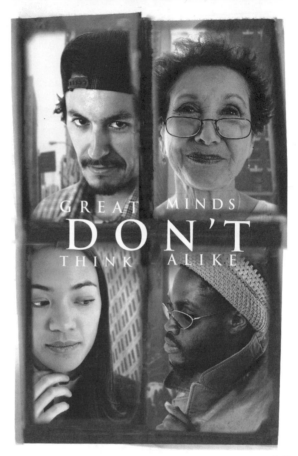

GREAT MINDS
D O N'T
THINK ALIKE

At Bell Atlantic we believe in the power of diversity and the power of the individual. It is individual thinking from a diverse group of people working together that provides fresh new ideas and gives us a competitive edge. At Bell Atlantic you're in good company.

s & Subway
Main
8-330-1234
ccess -Disabled
8-596-8585
reyhound
0-231-2222
lampton Jitney
0-936-0440

rries
Ellis Island
2-269-5755
larbor Shuttle
8-254-RIDE
JY Waterway–
0-53-FERRY
Staten Island
8-815-BOAT
Seastreak
0-262-8743
Statue of Liberty
2-269-5755

eorge
ashington Bridge
Js Station
2-564-1114

elicopter
Helicopter
light Services
2-355-0801
iberty
2-487-4777

K Airport
Main
8-244-4444
Train to Plane
8-858-7272

Guardia
rport
Main
8-533-3705

• Airport Bus
718-476-5353
• Ferry
800-53-FERRY
• Parking
718-533-3850

Newark
Airport
• Main
973-961-6000
• Airport Bus
973-242-0394
• Parking
973-961-4750

NY Passenger
Ship Terminal
212-246-5451

Port Authority
Bus Terminal
212-564-8484

Roosevelt
Island Tram
212-832-4543

Trains
• Amtrak
800-523-8720
212-582-6875
• Long Island
Railroad (LIRR)
718-217-5477
• Metro North
800-638-7646
• NJ Transit
800-626-7433
• PATH
800-234-7284

Teterboro
Airport
201-288-1775

BUSINESS &
CONSUMER
Better Business
Bureau
212-533-6200

Chambers of
Commerce
BK718-875-1000
BN 718-829-4111
MA 212-493-7400
QS 718-898-8500
SI 718-727-1900

Consumer Affairs
212-487-4444

Gas,Electric,
Water Complaints
800-342-3377

Small Business
Administration
(SBA)
212-264-4354

Taxi Complaints
212-221-8294

GOVERNMENT
Borough President
MA 212-669-8300

City Council
212-788-7100

Mayor's Office
212-788-7585

Tax Info
• City Tax (24hr)
718-935-6736
• Federal (IRS)
800-829-1040
• State Tax
800-225-5829

HEALTH &
HUMAN
AIDS Hotline
800-462-6787

Alcoholics
Anonymous
212-647-1680

All Night Pharmacy
Duane Reade
24 East 14 St,
212-989-3632

Bail 212-669-2879

Department
for the Aging
212-442-1000

Disabled Info
212-229-3000

Domestic
Violence Hotline
800-621-4673

Gay and Lesbian
Switchboard
212-777-1800

Health Info (24hr)
212-434-2000

Legal Aid Society
212-577-3300

Medicaid
718-291-1900

Medicare
800-638-6833

Salvation Army
212-337-7200

Senior Citizens
212-442-1000

Salvation Army
212-337-7200

Social Security
800-772-1213

LIBRARIES
NY Public
212-340-0849

NY Science,
Industry &
Business
(SIBL)
212-592-7001

PARKING &
TRAFFIC
Potholes
212-442-7942

Sidewalks
212-442-7942

Towed-Away?
212-869-2929

Registration Plates
212-645-5550

Parking Violations
718-422-7800

UTILITIES
ConEdison
800-75-CONED

Bell Atlantic
890-1550

WEBSITES NY
All internet
addresses listed
are assumed to
begin with "www."

Café los Negroes
losnegroes.com

Central Park
centralpark.org

Citysearch NY
citysearch.com

Metrobeat
metrobeat.com

Official City of
New York
Web Site
ci.nyc.ny.us/
home.html

NYC Reference
a.k.a.Clay Irving's
Home Page
panix.com/~clay/

The New York Times
nytimes.com

The New York Web
nyw.com

NYC Beer Guide
nycbeer.org

Total New York
totalny.com

VanDam, Inc.
vandam.com

Village Voice
villagevoice.com

NOTES:

ATTRACTIONS

ATTRACTIONS

Abyssinian Baptist Church
132 W 138 St,
212-862-7474 **149B**

The Apollo Theater
253 W 125 St,
212-749-5838 **149C**

Battery Park City Esplanade **102A**

Bloomingdale's
1000 Third Av,
212-705-2000 **130D**

Brooklyn Bridge
@ City Hall Park, or
Adams St, BK **105A**

Carnegie Hall
881 Seventh Av,
212-247-7800 **125A**

Cathedral Church of St. John the Divine
Amsterdam Av @ 112 St,
212-662-2133 **144D**

Central Park **129A**

Circle Line
W 42 St @ 12 Av,
212-563-3200 **120A**

Carnegie Hall
881 Seventh Av,
212-247-7800 **125A**

Chelsea Piers
Joe Di Maggio Hwy @ 23 St
212-336-6666 **116C**

Chinatown **107C**

Chrysler Bldg
E 42 St @
Lexington Av **126D**

Citicorp Center
W 53 St @
Lexington Av, **126B**

The Cloisters
Fort Tryon Pk,
212-923-3700 **158B**

Columbia University
W 116 St @ Broadway,
212-854-1754 **144B**

Ellis Island
Ferry from Battery Pk
212-363-3200 **102C**

Empire State Bldg
350 Fifth Av,
212-736-3100 **121D**

F.A.O. Schwarz
767 Fifth Av,
212-644-9400 **129D**

Federal Hall Nat'l Memorial
26 Wall St,
212-264-8711 **103A**

Federal Reserve Bank of NY
33 Liberty St,
212-720-6130 **105C**

Flatiron Bldg
Fifth Av @ 23 St, **117B**

Grant National Memorial
Riverside Dr @ W 122 St,
212-666-1640 **144A**

Lincoln Center for the Performing Arts
Broadway @ 65 St,
212-875-5000 **128D**

Little Italy
Mulberry St **107A**

Macy's Herald Sq
151 W 34 St,
212-695-4400 **121C**

Madison Sq Garden
4 Penn Plz,
212-465-6741 **121C**

Meatmarket **112A**

Morris-Jumel Mansion
65 Jumel Ter,
212-923-8008 **154D**

NBC Studio Tour
30 Rockefeller Plz,
212-664-4000 **125D**

New York Public Library (NYPL)
42 St @ 5 Av,
212-661-7220 **122A**

New York Stock Exchange (NYSE)
20 Broad St,
212-656-5165 **102A**

The Plaza Hotel
768 Fifth Av ,
212-759-3000 **129D**

Radio City Music Hall
Sixth Av @ W 50 St,
212-247-4777 **125B**

Riverside Church
490 Riverside Dr
212-222-5900 **144A**

Rockefeller Center
Fifth–Sixth Avs & 48–51 Sts,
212-698-2950 **125D**

St Patrick's Cathedral
Fifth Av @ E 50 St ,
212-753-2261 **125B**

St Paul's Chapel
B'way @ Fulton St,
212-602-0872 **104D**

Seagram Bldg
375 Park Av,
212-572-7000 **126B**

Sony Wonder Technology Lab
550 Madison Av @ 56 St,
212-833-8100 **126B**

SoHo
6 Av–B'way, Houston –Canal Sts **109D**

Statue of Liberty Liberty Island
212-363-3200 Ferry,
212-269-5755 **102C**

Theodore Roosevelt Birthplace
28 E 20 St,
212-260-1616 **118C**

Tiffany & Co.
727 Fifth Av,
212-755-8000 **126A**

Times Square
46 St & B'way **125C**

Trinity Church
89 B'way @ Wall St,
212-602-0872 **102A**

Trump Tower
725 Fifth Av @ E 56 St,
212-832-2000 **126A**

United Nations
First Av @ E 45 St,
212-963-1234 **127C**

Waldorf–Astoria
301 Park Av,
212-355-3000 **126B**

Warner Bros. Studio Store
Fifth Av @ 57 St,
718-754-0300 **129**

Washington Square Park, **11**

Woolworth Bldg
233 Broadway **104**

World Financial Center (WFC)
Liberty St @ the Hudson River,
212-945-0505 **104**

World Trade Cente
WTC 2 @ Liberty S
212-435-7000 **104**

MUSEUMS

Abigail Adams Smith House Museum
421 E 61 St,
212-838-6878 **131**

African–American Wax Museum
316 W 115 St,
212-678-7818 **14 **

Alternative Museum
594 Broadway #40
212-966-4444 **109**

American Craft Museum
40 W 53 St,
212-956-6047 **125**

American Museum of Natural History
CPW @ 79 St,
212-769-5000 **133**

MUSEUMS 3

...erican ...mismatic ...ciety
...dubon Ter,
...2-234-3130 **152B**

...e Americas ...ciety
... Park Av,
...-249-8950 **130B**

...e Asia Society
... Park Av,
...-249-6400 **130B**

...ian American ... Centre
... Bowery,
...-233-2154 **107C**

...e Black Fashion ...seum
... W 126 St,
...-666-1320 **149D**

...ildren's Museum ...Manhattan
... W 83 St,
...-721-1223 **132B**

...ina Institute ...America
... E 65 St,
...-744-8181 **130B**

...e Cloisters
...t Tryon Pk,
...-923-3700 **158B**

...oper-Hewitt ...tional ...sign ...seum
... 91 St,
...-849-8300 **137D**

...hesh Museum
... Fifth Av,
...-759-0606 **125D**

Dia Center for the Arts
548 W 22 St,
212-989-5912 **116B**

The Drawing Center
35 Wooster St,
212-219-2166 **109D**

El Museo del Barrio
1230 Fifth Av,
212-831-7272 **141B**

Exit Art / 1st World
548 Broadway,
212-966-7745 **109B**

Forbes Magazine Galleries
62 Fifth Av,
212-206-5548 **113A**

Fraunces Tavern Museum
54 Pearl St,
212-425-1778 **103A**

Frick Collection
1 E 70 St,
212-288-0700 **130B**

Guggenheim (SoHo)
575 Broadway @ Prince St,
212-423-3500 **109B**

The Hispanic Society of America
613 W 155 St,
212-690-0743 **152B**

Int'l Center of Photography (ICP)
1135 Fifth Av,
212-860-1777 **137B**

ICP Midtown
6 Av @ W 43 St,
212-768-4680 **125D**

Intrepid Sea-Air-Space Museum
W 46 St @ 12 Av,
212-245-0072 **124C**

Japan Society
333 E 47 St,
212-832-1155 **126D**

Jewish Museum
1109 Fifth Av
(E 92 St),
212-423-3200 **137B**

Lower East Side Tenement Museum
90 Orchard St,
212-431-0233 **110B**

The Metropolitan Museum of Art
5 Av @ E 82 St,
212-535-7710 **133B**

Morgan Library
29 E 36 St,
212-685-0610 **122B**

Museum for African Art
593 Broadway,
212-966-1313 **109B**

Museum of Amer. Financial History
28 Broadway,
212-908-4110 **102B**

Museum of American Folk Art
2 Lincoln Sq,
212-977-7298 **128B**

Museum of Amer. Illustration
128 E 63 St,
212-838-2560 **130D**

Museum of the City of New York
1220 Fifth Av,
212-534-1672 **141B**

Museum of Chinese in the Americas
70 Mulberry St,
212-619-4785 **107C**

The Museum of Jewish Heritage
18 First Pl,
212-968-1800 **102D**

Museum of Modern Art (MoMA)
11 W 53 St,
212-708-9480 **125B**

The Museum of Television & Radio
25 W 52 St,
212-621-6600 **125B**

Nat'l Museum of the American Indian
Customs House @ Bowling Green,
212-825-6700 **102D**

Nat'l Academy Museum
1083 Fifth Av @ E 89 St,
212-369-4880 **137B**

New Museum of Contemporary Art
583 Broadway,
212-219-1222 **109B**

NYC Fire Museum
278 Spring St,
212-691-1303 **109C**

New–York Historical Society
170 CPW,
212-873-3400 **133C**

Newseum NY
580 Madison Av,
212-317-7503 **126B**

Police Museum
235 E 20 St,
212-477-9753 **118D**

Rose Center for Earth & Science
CPW @ W 81 St,
212-769-5900 **133A**

Skyscraper Museum
16 Wall St,
212-766-1324 **102B**

Solomon R Guggenheim Museum (Uptown)
1071 Fifth Av,
212-423-3500 **138C**

South Street Seaport Museum
Seaport Plz
207 Front St,
212-748-8600 **105C**

Studio Museum in Harlem
144 W 125 St,
212-864-4500 **145B**

Ukrainian Museum
203 Second Av,
212-228-0110 **114A**

Whitney Museum of American Art
945 Madison Av,
212-570-3600 **134D**

Whitney Museum at Philip Morris
120 Park Av,
212-878-2550 **122B**

TO FIND A TOP 100

Simply turn to page and locate the attraction in grids A,B,C or D.

BUSINESS

ADVERTISING

WPP Group USA
309 W 49 St,
212-632-2200 **125C**

Ogilvy & Mather
309 W 49 St,
212-237-4000 **125C**

Saatchi & Saatchi
375 Hudson St,
212-463-2000 **108B**

OmniCom Group
437 Madison Av,
212-415-3600 **130D**

**Interpublic Group
of Companies**
1271 Sixth Av,
212-399-8000 **126A**

**CONSUMER
GOODS**

Avon
1345 Sixth Av,
212-282-5000 **126A**

**Bristol-Meyers
Squibb Company**
345 Park Av,
212-546-4000 **126B**

Colgate Palmolive
300 Park Av,
212-310-2000 **126D**

Estée Lauder
767 Fifth Av,
212-572-4200 **129D**

Kinney Shoe Corp
233 Broadway,
212-720-3700 **104B**

Pfizer
235 E 42 St,
212-573-2323 **123A**

MAFCO
36 E 63 St,
212-688-9000 **130D**

Philip Morris
120 Park Av,
212-880-5000 **122B**

RJR Nabisco
1301 Sixth Av,
212-258-5600 **126A**

Seagram
375 Park Av,
212-572-7000 **126B**

Unilever
390 Park Av,
212-888-1260 **126B**

Venator Group, Inc.
233 Broadway,
212-553-2000 **104D**

FASHION

Donna Karan
550 Seventh Av,
212-640-2000 **121A**

Calvin Klein
205 W 39 St,
212-719-2600 **121A**

Ralph Lauren
650 Madison Av,
212-318-7000 **130D**

**FINANCIAL
SERVICES**

American Express
200 Vesey St,
212-640-2000 **104C**

Bank of NY
48 Wall St,
212-495-1784 **103A**

Bear Stearns
245 Park Av,
212-272-2000 **126D**

**Chase
Manhattan Bank**
270 Park Av,
212-270-6000 **126D**

Citigroup
153 E 53 St,
212-559-1000 **126B**

Transamerica
350 Park Av,
212-223-3200 **126B**

Deutsche Bank
31 West 52 St,
212-469-8000 **126A**

**Donaldson, Lufkin
& Jenrette**
277 Park Av,
212-892-3000 **126D**

Ernst & Young
787 Seventh Av,
212-773-3000 **125A**

**Federal Reserve
Bank of NY**
33 Liberty St,
212-720-5000 **105C**

Fortis
1 Chase Manhattan Plz,
212-859-7000 **103A**

Goldman Sachs
85 Broad St,
212-902-1000 **103A**

HSBC
140 Broadway,
212-658-1028 **104D**

**KPMG Peat
Marwick**
345 Park Av,
212-758-9700 **126B**

JP Morgan
60 Wall St,
212-483-2323 **103A**

Lehman Brothers
3 WFC
@ 200 Vesey St,
212-526-7000 **104D**

Merrill Lynch
N & S Tower, WFC, ,
212-449-1000 **104C**

**Morgan Stanley,
Dean Witter,
Discover & Co**
1585 Broadway,
212-761-3000 **125C**

PaineWebber Group
1285 Sixth Av,
212-713-3000 **125B**

**Prudential
Securities**
199 Water St,
212-214-1000 **105C**

Republic Nat'l Bank
452 Fifth Av,
212-525-5000 **122A**

**Salomon Brothers
Smith Barney**
388 Greenwich St,
212-816-6000 **106C**

INSURANCE

**Empire Blue Cross
& Blue Shield**
622 Third Av,
212-476-1000 **122B**

The Equitable
1290 Sixth Av,
212-554-1234 **125A**

Guardian Life
201 Park Av S,
212-598-8000 **118D**

Marsh & McLennan
1166 Sixth Av,
212-345-5000 **126C**

Met Life
1 Madison Av,
212-578-2211 **11**

Mutual Life of NY
1740 Broadway,
212-708-2000 **12**

NYLCare Health Pla
1 Liberty Plz,
212-437-1000 **10**

NY Life
51 Madison Av,
212-576-7000 **11**

**Teachers Insuran
& Annuity Assoc.**
730 Third Av,
212-490-9000 **12**

**Reliance Group
Holdings**
55 E 52 St, MA
212-909-1100 **12**

Travelers Group
388 Greenwich St,
212-816-8000 **10**

MEDIA

ABC
77 W 66 St,
212-456-7777 **12**

Bertelsmann
1540 Broadway,
212-782-1000 **12**

CBS
51 W 52 St,
212-975-4321 **12**

FOX
205 E 67 St,
212-452-5555 **13**

Hearst
959 Eighth Av,
212-649-2000 **12**

BUSINESS

·C
Rockefeller Plz,
2-664-4000 **125D**

·ws America ·ldings
·1 Sixth Av,
2-852-7000 **125D**

·ny Corp
·) Madison Av,
2-833-6800 **126B**

·ne Warner
·Rockefeller Plz, ·
2-484-8000 **125B**

·rner Corporation
·5 Hudson St,
2-229-6000 **108B**

·com
·5 Broadway,
2-258-6000 **125C**

·BLISHING

·vance ·blications
·imes Sq,
2-286-2860 **125C**

·rnes & Noble
·2 Fifth Av,
2-633-3300 **118C**

·ndé Nast
·imes Sq,
2-286-2860 **125C**

·in's NY Business
·1 E 42 St,
2-210-0100 **122A**

·w Jones
·1 Liberty St,
2-416-2000 **102B**

·bes
·Fifth Av,
2-620-2200 **113A**

Gruner & Jahr
375 Lexington Av,
212-499-2000 **122B**

Hyperion
77 W 66 St,
212-456-7777 **129A**

HarperCollins
10 E 53 St,
212-207-7000 **126B**

Hachette Filipacchi
1633 Broadway,
212-767-6000 **125A**

Hearst Books
1350 Sixth Av,
212-261-6500 **126A**

Hearst Magazines
250 W 55 St,
212-649-4129 **126A**

McGraw Hill
1221 Sixth Av,
212-512-2000 **125A**

New York Times
229 W 43 St.
212-556-1234 **125A**

Newsweek
251 W 57 St.
212445-4000 **129C**

Penguin–Putnam
375 Hudson St,
212-366-2000 **109A**

Random House
1540 Broadway,
212-354-6500 **125C**

St. Martin's Press
175 Fifth Av,
212-674-5151 **118A**

Simon & Schuster
1230 Sixth Av,
212-698-7000 **125D**

von Holtzbrinck
115 W 18 St,
212-367-0100 **117D**

Warner Books
1271 Sixth Av,
212-522-7200 **125A**

REAL ESTATE
Cushman Wakefield
51 W 52 St,
212-841-7500 **125B**

Durst Organization
1155 Sixth Av,
212-789-1155 **125D**

Helmsley–Spear
60 E 42 St,
212-687-6400 **122B**

Loew's
667 Madison Av,
212-545-2000 **130D**

Mitsui & Company USA
200 Park Av,
212-878-4000 **126D**

Newmark
1501 Broadway,
212-354-2500 **125C**

Trump Organization
725 Fifth Av,
212-832-2000 **126B**

TECHNOLOGY
AT&T
32 Sixth Av,
212-387-5400 **106B**

Bell Atlantic
1095 Sixth Av,
212-395-2121 **126C**

Dover Corp.
280 Park Av,
212-922-1640 **126D**

ITT Corp
1330 Sixth Av,
212-258-1000 **126A**

Mitsubishi Int'l
520 Madison Av,
212-605-2000 **126B**

Nissho Iwai
1211 Sixth Av,
212-704-6500 **125A**

Philips Electronics
100 E 42 St,
212-850-5000 **122B**

Siemens
1301 Sixth Av,
212-258-4000 **126A**

Toshiba America
1251 Sixth Av,
212-596-0600 **125A**

UTILITIES & TRANSPORT
Bell Atlantic
1095 Sixth Av,
212-395-2121 **121B**

Con Edison
4 Irving Pl,
212-460-4600 **118D**

MTA
347 Madison Av,
212-878-7000 **126D**

BUSINESS IMPROVEMENT DISTRICTS (BIDS)
Alliance for Downtown, NY
120 Broadway,
212-566-6700 **102B**

Fashion Center
249 W 39 St,
212-764-9600 **121A**

Fifth Av
600 Fifth Av,
212-265-1310 **126C**

Grand Central Partnership
6 E 43 St,
212-818-1777 **122A**

Lincoln Square
10 Columbus Cir,
212-974-9100 **129C**

Madison Av
903 Madison Av,
212-249-4095 **130B**

Times Square
1560 Broadway,
212-768-1560 **125C**

14 St/Union Square
223 E 14 St,
212-674-1164 **118D**

34 St Partnership
6 E 43 St,
212-818-1913 **122A**

CHAMBERS OF COMMERCE
NYC Partnership
1 Battery Park Plz,
212-493-7400 **121C**

CONVENTIONS
Jacob Javits
11 Av @ 36 St,
212-216-2000 **120A**

NY Coliseum
10 Columbus Cir,
212-757-3440 **129C**

NY Convention Pier
Pier 92, **124A**

TO FIND A TOP 100

Simply turn to page
and locate the
company in grids
A,B,C or D.

DINING

AMERICAN
Aureole $$$$
34 E 61 St,
212-319-1660 **130D**

The Coach House $$$$
16 E 32 St,
212-696-1800 **122D**

Eleven Madison Park $$$$
11 Madison Av,
212-889-0905 **118A**

Gramercy Tavern $$$$
42 E 20 St,
212-477-0777 **118D**

March $$$$
405 E 58 St,
212-754-6272 **131C**

Tribeca Grill $$$
375 Greenwich St,
212-941-3900 **106C**

Union Sq Cafe $$$$
21 E 16 St,
212-243-4020 **118C**

BELGIAN
Markt $$$
401 W 14 St,
212-727-3314 **116D**

BISTRO
Balthazar $$$
80 Spring St,
212-965-1414 **109B**

Pastis $$$
9 Ninth Av,
212-929-4844 **112B**

Raoul's $$$
180 Prince St,
212-966-3518 **109A**

CHINESE
Canton $$$
45 Division St,
212-226-4441 **107C**

Chin Chin $$$
216 E 49 St,
212-888-4555 **127C**

Joe's Shanghai $$
9 Pell St (Mott St),
212-233-8888 **107C**

Shun Lee Palace $$$
155 E 55 St,
212-371-8844 **126B**

Tse Yang $$$
34 E 51 St,
212-688-5447 **126B**

20 Mott St $$$
20 Mott St (Pell St)
212-964-0380 **107C**

CONTINENTAL
Four Seasons $$$$
99 E 52 St,
212-754-9494 **126B**

Marylou's $$$
21 W 9 St,
212-533-0012 **113A**

One if by Land, TIBS $$$$
17 Barrow St,
212-228-0822 **113C**

Petrossian $$$$
182 W 58 St,
212-245-2214 **130C**

Peacock Alley $$$
Waldorf-Astoria
301 Park Av,
212-872-4895 **126D**

21 Club $$$$
21 W 52 St,
212-582-7200 **125B**

DELI/KOSHER
Barney Greengrass $
541 Amsterdam Av, ,
212-724-4707
136D

Carnegie Deli $
854 Seventh Av,
212-757-2245 **125A**

Katz's $
205 E Houston St,
212-254-2246 **110B**

Ratners $$
138 Delancy St,
212-677-5588 **110B**

2nd Av Deli $
156 Second Av,
212-677-0606 **114A**

DINER
Bright Food Shop $$
218 Eighth Av,
212-243-4433
117A

Coffee Shop $$
29 Union Sq W,
212-243-7969 **118C**

EJ's Luncheonette $$
447 Amsterdam Av,
212-873-3444 **132B**

Empire Diner $$
210 Tenth Av,
212-243-2736 **116B**

Market Diner $$
572 Eleventh Av,
212-695-0415 **120B**

Vynl Diner $
824 Ninth Av,
212-974-2003 **124B**

DOMINICAN
Cafe Con Leche $
424 Amsterdam Av,
212-595-7000 **132B**

FRENCH
Bouley Bakery $$$$
120 W Bway,
212-964-2525 **106D**

Daniel $$$$
20 E 76 St,
212-982-6930 **134D**

Chanterelle $$$$$
2 Harrison St,
212-966-6960 **104B**

La Côte Basque $$$$
60 W 55 St,
212-688-6525 **126A**

Le Cirque 2000 $$$$
455 Madison Av,
212-303-7788 **126B**

La Luncheonette $$$
130 10 Av,
212-675-0342 **116D**

Les Célébrités $$$$
155 W 58 St,
212-484-5113 **129C**

Jean Claude $$
137 Sullivan St,
212-475-9232 **109A**

FUN FOOD
Brooklyn Diner USA $$
212 W 57 St,
212-581-8900 **125A**

Hard Rock Cafe $
221 W 57 St,
212-489-6565 **12**

Official All Star C
$$ 1540 B'way,
212-840-TEAM **12**

Tavern on the Gre
$$$ CPW & 67 St,
212-873-3200 **12**

FUSION
Cendrillon $$
45 Mercer St,
212-343-9012 **1**

Jo Jo $$$
160 E 64 St,
212-223-5656 **13**

Verbena $$$
54 Irving Pl,
212-260-5454 **1**

Mesa Grill $$$
102 Fifth Av,
212-807-7400 **1**

GREEK/MIDDL
EASTERN
Agrotikon $$
322 E 14 St,
212-473-2602 **1**

Periyali $$$
35 W 20 St,
212-463-7890 **1**

Habib's Place $
438 E 9 St,
212-979-2243 **1**

INDIAN
Baluchi's $$
193 Spring St,
212-226-2828 **1**

DINING

y Leaf *SS*
V 56 St,
2-957-1818 **125B**

wat *SSS*
) E 58 St,
2-355-7555 **131C**

bla *SS*
Madison Av,
2-889-0667 **118A**

aan *SSS*
W 48 St,
2-977-8400 **125B**

ALIAN
bbo *SSS*
) Waverly Place,
2-777-0303 **113C**

ffé Bondi *SSS*
V 20 St,
2-691-8136 **117D**

l Legno *S*
E 9 St,
2-7774-650 **114A**

idia *SSSS*
3 E 58 St,
2-758-1479 **131C**

Giglio *SSS*
Warren St,
2-571-5555 **104B**

Mulino *SSSS*
W 3 St,
2-673-3783 **113C**

Nido *SSS*
E 53 St,
2-753-8450 **127A**

Trattoria dell'Arte
SSS 900 7Av,
212-245-9800 **125A**

JAPANESE
Hasaki *SS*
210 E 9 St,
212-473-3327 **114A**

Iso *SS*
175 Second Av,
212-777-0361 **115C**

Nobu *SSSS*
105 Hudson St, 212-
219-0500 **106C**

Tomoe Sushi *S*
172 Thompson St,
212-777-9346 **113C**

NUEVO MEXICANO
Santa Fe *SS*
72 W 69 St,
212-724-0822 **129A**

Zarela *SSS*
953 Second Av,
212-644-6740 **127C**

Rocking Horse Cafe
Mexicano *SS*
182 Eighth Av,
212-463-9511 **117C**

OLDE NEW YORK
Café des Artistes
SSS 1 W 67 St,
212-877-3500 **129A**

Fanelli *S*
94 Prince St,
212-226-9412 **109B**

Old Homestead *SSS*
56 Ninth Av,
212-242-9040 **117C**

PIZZA
Joe's Pizza *S*
233 Bleecker St,
212-366-1182 **113C**

John's Pizzeria *S*
278 Bleecker St,
212-243-1680 **113C**

Lombardi's *SS*
32 Spring St,
212-941-7994 **110C**

RUSSIAN
Russian Tea Room
SSSS 150 W 57 St,
212-974-2111 **125B**

The Firebird *SSSS*
365 W 46 St,
212-586-0244 **125C**

SEAFOOD
Aquagrill *SSS*
210 Spring St,
212-274-0505 **109A**

Le Bernardin *SSSS*
155 W 51 St,
212-489-1515 **125A**

Le Pescadou *SSS*
18 King St,
212-924-3434 **108A**

Oceana *SSSS*
55 E 54 St,
212-759-5941 **126B**

SPANISH/TAPAS
Bolo *SSS*
23 E 22 St,
212-228-2200 **118A**

El Cid *SS*
322 W 15 St,
212-929-9332 **117C**

Marichu *SSS*
342 E 46 St,
212-370-1866 **127C**

STEAK
Palm & Palm Too
SSS 837 Second Av,
212-687-2953 **127C**

Post House *SSSS*
28 E 23 St,
212-935-2888 **130D**

Smith & Wollensky
SSS 797 Third Av,
212-753-1530 **126D**

Sparks *SSSS*
210 E 46 St,
212-687-4855 **127C**

THAI
Jai-Ya Thai *SS*
396 Third Av,
212-889-1330 **118B**

Vong *SSS*
200 E 54 St,
212-486-9592 **127A**

TROPICAL
Asia de Cuba *SSS*
237 Madison Av,
212-726-7755 **122B**

Bambou *SSS*
243 E 14 St,
212-505-1180 **118D**

Campo *SS*
89 Greenwich Av,
212-691-8080 **112C**

Calle Ocho *SSS*
466 Columbus Av
(81/82 Sts),
212-873-5025 **132B**

Circus *SSS*
808 Lexington Av,
212-223-2965 **130D**

Tropica *SSS*
200 Park Av,
212-867-6767 **126D**

Casa Brasil *SS*
316 E 53 St,
212-355-5360 **127A**

VEGETARIAN
Angelica Kitchen *S*
300 E 12 St,
212-228-2909 **114A**

Hangawi *SSS*
12 E 32 St,
212-213-0077 **122C**

Mavalli Palace *SS*
46 E 29 St,
212-679-5535 **118B**

Quantum Leap *S*
88 W 3 St,
212-677-8050 **113C**

Souen *SS*
28 E 13 St,
212-627-7150 **113B**

VIETNAMNESE
Le Colonial *SSS*
149 E 57 St,
212-752-0808 **130D**

Monsoon *SSS*
435 Amsterdam Av,
212-580-8686 **132B**

VIEWS
Windows on the
World *SSSS*
1 WTC 107th fl,
212-524-7011 **104A**

TO FIND A TOP 100

Simply turn to page
and locate the
restaurant in grids
A,B,C or D.

HOTELS

BED & BREAKFAST
All B & B's require reservations prior to arrival.

The Gracie Inn $$
502 E 81 St,
212-628-1700 **135**B

The Inn at Irving Pl
$$$ 56 Irving Place
212-533-4600 **118**A

SoHo $$
167 Crosby St,
212-925-1034 **114**C

Upper West Side $$
W 77 St,
212-472-2000 **132**B

MANHATTAN
Downtown
Best Western Seaport Inn $$
33 Peck Slip,
212-766-6600 **105**C

Holiday Inn Downtown $$
138 Lafayette St,
212-966-8898 **106**A

Holiday Inn Wall Street District
$$$ 15 Gold St,
212-232-7700 **105**C

Marriott Financial Center
$$$ 85 West St,
212-385-4900 **102**B

Marriott WTC, New York $$$
3 WTC,
212-938-9100 **104**D

The Millenium Hilton $$$
55 Church St,
800-835-2220 **104**D

Regent Wall Street
$$$$$ 55 Wall St,
212-308-0601 **103**A

SoHo & The Village
The Larchmont $
27 W 11 St,
212-989-9333 **113**A

The Mercer $$$
99 Prince St,
212-966-6060 **109**B

Off-SoHo Suites $
11 Rivington St,
212-979-9808 **110**A

SoHo Grand $$$
310 W Broadway,
212-965-3000 **106**B

Washington Sq $
103 Waverly Pl,
212-777-9515 **113**A

Chelsea & Gramercy Park
Chelsea Hotel $$
222 W 23 St,
212-243-3700 **117**A

Chelsea Int'l Youth Hostel $
251 W 20 St,
212-647-0010 **117**C

Chelsea Savoy $$
204 W 23 St,
212-929-9353 **117**A

Gramercy Park $$
2 Lexington Av,
800-221-4083 **118**B

Southgate Tower $$
371 Seventh Av,
212-563-1800 **121**C

Midtown East
Beekman Tower $$
3 Mitchell Pl,
212-355-7300 **127**C

The Benjamin $$$$
125 E 50 St,
212-753-2700 **126**B

Crowne Plaza at the United Nations
$$ 304 E 42 St,
212-986-8800 **123**A

The Delmonico $$$
502 Park Av,
212-355-2500 **130**D

The Doral Park Av
$$ 70 Park Av,
212-687-7050 **122**B

Dumont Plaza Suite
$$$ 150 E 34 St,
800-ME-SUITE **122**D

Eastgate Tower Suite
$$ 222 E 39 St,
800-ME-SUITE **123**A

The Fitzpatrick $$$
687 Lexington Av,
212-355-0100 **126**B

The Four Seasons
$$$$$ 57 E 57 St,
212-758-5700 **130**D

Grand Hyatt NY $$$
Park Av @ 42 St,
800-228-9000 **122**B

Helmsley Middletowne $$
148 E 48 St,
800-221-4982 **126**C

Hotel Élysée $$
60 E 54 St,
212-753-1066 **126**B

Hotel Inter-Continental NY $$$
111 E 48 St,
800-327-0200 **126**D

Kitano $$$$
66 Park Av,
212-885-7000 **122**B

Loews NY $$
569 Lexington Av,
212-752-7000 **126**B

Morgans $$$
237 Madison Av,
800-334-3408 **122**D

The New Yorker $
481 Eighth Av,
212-301-2285 **121**C

NY Helmsley $$$
212 E 42 St,
800-221-4982 **122**B

The New York Palace $$$$
445 Madison Av,
212-888-7000 **126**B

Omni Berkshire Place
$$$ 21 E 52 St,
800-THE-OMNI **125**B

Pickwick Arms $$
230 51 St,
212-355-0300 **127**A

Regal UN Plaza
$$$$ 1 UN Plz,
800-222-8888 **127**C

The Roger Williams
$$$ 131 Madison Av,
212-488-7000 **122**D

Roger Smith $$
501 Lexington Av,
212-755-1400 **12**

Roosevelt Hotel $
45 East 45 St,
212-661-9600 **12**

St Regis $$$$$
2 E 55 St,
800-759-7550 **12**

San Carlos $$
150 E 50 St,
800-722-2012 **12**

Shelburne $$
303 Lexington Av,
800-689-5200 **12**

Sheraton Russell
$$$ 45 Park Av,
212-685-7676 **12**

Swissôtel, the Drake
$$$ 440 Park Av,
800-63SWISS **12**

Vanderbilt YMCA
224 E 47 St,
212-756-9600 **12**

The "W" Court $$
130 E 39 St
212-685-1100 **12**

The "W" NY $$$
541 Lexington Av,
212-755-1200 **12**

The "W" Tuscany
$$$ 120 E 39 St,
212-686-1600 **12**

The Waldorf–Astoria
$$$ 301 Park Av,
800-WALDORF **12**

The Waldorf Towers
$$$$$ 100 E 50 St.
800-WALDORF **12**

HOTELS

Midtown West

The Algonquin $$$
9 W 44 St,
800-548-0345 **125D**

Best Western President $
34 W 48 St,
800-826-4667 **125C**

Doubletree Guest Suites $$$
568 Broadway,
212-719-1600 **126C**

Essex House–Nikko $$$ 160 CPS,
800-NIKKO-US **129C**

Hampshire Ambassador $
132 W 45 St,
212-961-7600 **125C**

Hotel Edison $
228 W 47 St,
212-840-5000 **125C**

Quality Hotel & Suites $
9 W 46 St,
212-719-2300 **125D**

Holiday Inn Crowne Plaza $$$$
1605 Broadway,
800-227-6963 **125A**

The Iroquois $$$
9 W 44 St,
212-840-3080 **125D**

The Mansfield $$
12 W 44 St,
212-944-6050 **125D**

The Manhattan $$
7 W 32 St,
212-736-1600 **121C**

Marriott Marquis $$$ 1535 B'way,
800-228-9290 **125C**

Michelangelo $$$
152 W 51 St,
800-237-0990 **125A**

Millenium Broadway $$$
145 W 44 St,
800-622-5569 **125C**

The NY Hilton $$$
1335 Sixth Av,
800-HILTONS **125B**

Paramount $$
235 W 46 St,
800-225-7474 **124C**

The Peninsula $$
700 Fifth Av,
212-736-5000 **126A**

Le Parker Meridien $$$ 118 W 57 St,
800-543-4300 **125B**

The Peninsula NY $$$$ 700 Fifth Av,
800-262-9467 **126A**

The Plaza $$$
768 Fifth Av,
800-759-3000 **129D**

Quality Inn Midtown $ 157 W 47 St,
800-826-4667 **125C**

RIHGA Royal $$$
151 W 54 St,
800-937-5454 **125A**

The Royalton $$$
44 W 44 St,
800-635-9013 **125D**

St Moritz on-the-Park $$$ 50 CPS,
800-221-4774 **129D**

Park Central Hotel $$$ 870 Seventh Av,
212-247-8000 **125A**

Sheraton New York Hotel & Towers $$
811 Seventh Av,
800-325-3535 **125A**

The Shoreham $$$
33 W 54 St,
212-247-6700 **125B**

The Warwick $$$
65 W 54 St,
212-247-2700 **125B**

Westin Central Park $$$$ 112 CPS,
212-757-1900 **129D**

The Wyndham $$
42 W 58 St,
212-753-3500 **129D**

Upper Eastside

The Carlyle $$$$
35 E 76 St,
212-744-1600 **134D**

The Franklin $$
164 E 87 St,
212-369-1000 **139C**

Plaza Athénée $$$$
37 E 64 St,
800-734-9100 **130D**

The Lowell $$$$
28 E 63 St,
800-221-4444 **130D**

The Mark $$$$
25 E 77 St,
800-THE-MARK **133D**

The Regency $$$$
540 Park Av,
212-759-4100 **130D**

The Pierre $$$$
5 Av @ E 61 St,
800-332-3442 **129D**

Sherry–Netherland $$$$$ 781 Fifth Av, ,
800-247-4377 **129D**

The Stanhope $$$$ 995 Fifth Av,
800-828-1123 **133B**

Surrey $$
20 E 76 St,
212-288-3700 **133D**

The Wales $$$
1295 Madison Av,
212-876-6000 **138B**

92nd St YMCA de Hirsch Residence $ 1395 Lexington Av,
800-858-4692 **139A**

Upper Westside

Beacon Hotel $$
2130 Broadway,
800-572-4969 **132D**

The Empire $$
44 W 63 St,
212-265-7400 **128D**

Inn New York City $$ 266 W 71 St,
212-580-1900 **128B**

Mayflower Hotel on the Park $$
15 Central Park W,
800-223-4164 **129C**

NY Int'l American Youth Hostel $
891 Amsterdam Av,
212-932-2300 **140D**

Trump International Hotel & Tower $$$$$
1 Central Park West,
800-44TRUMP **129C**

63rd St YMCA $
5 W 63 St,
212-787-4400 **129C**

RESERVATIONS

At Home in NY
800-692-4262

City Lights B & B
212-737-7049

NY by Phone
888-NYC-APPLE

New World
800-443-3800

Urban Ventures
212-594-5650

TO FIND A TOP 100

Simply turn to page and locate the hotels in grids A, B, C or D.

PRICE KEY

$ = less than $100
$$ = $100-$200
$$$ = $200-$300
$$$$ = $300-$400
$$$$$ = $400-$500

Price ranges given are for single occupancy midweek. It's smart to call for weekend specials and promotional rates.

NATURE & 3

CEMETERIES
African Burial
Grounds 104A
St Paul's 104D
Trinity 152B

Community
*Through fortitude
and grit, New
Yorkers have taken
over 700 vacant lots
and transformed
them into beautiful
and productive
gardens that help
strengthen their
communities.*

*Aided by Green
Thumb, city garden-
ers get access to
city land and horti-
cultural training.
Here are a few of
the finest in the five
boroughs.*

Brisas La Caribe
237 E 3 St, ...114D

6th & B
624 E 6 St, ...115A

Special
Biblical Garden
Cathedral Church of
St John the Divine,
........................144D

Cloisters
Ft Tryon Pk,
........................158B

Peace
UN Plz, ...127C

Conservatory
Central Pk, ...141B

St Luke's-in-the-Field
487 Hudson St,
........................112D

Shakespeare
Central Park,
........................133A

Strawberry Fields
Central Park,
........................129A

**INTERPRETIVE
CENTERS**
**Charles A Dana
Discovery**
Lenox Av & 110 St,
212-860-1370   141B

**Henry Luce
Nature Observatory**
Belvedere Castle
Central Park,
212-772-0210   133A

Urban Ecology
Inwood Pk,
212-304-2365   160B

PARKS
Battery 102D
Bennett 156B
Bryant................122A
Carl Schurz 139D
Central 129A-142A
Chelsea 116B
City Hall 105C
Columbus..........105A
Corlears Hook 111D
Damrosch 128D
De Witt
  Clinton 124A
East River 111B
East River
  Esplanade 123A
Frederick Johnson

........................153A
Fort Tryon..........158D
Fort Washington ......
........................156C
Gateway............131C
Gramercy..........118D
Inwood Hill 160D
Isham 161C
Hamilton Fish ..111A
Harlem River Drive..
........................153D-159A
Hell's Kitchen ..124D
High Bridge 154B
Hudson Sq 106A
Jackie Robinson
........................153C
James J. Walker
........................108B
Jeanette............103C
John Jay 135D
J Wood
  Wright............156D
Liberty 102B
Luis Cuvillier ..147A
Madison Sq......117B
Marcus Garvey ......
........................146B
Morningside 144B
Paley 126B
Randalls Is 302B
Riverbank State 148A
Riverside ....
........................132A-144A
Robert Moses ..123A
Robert F Wagner Jr.
........................102D
Rockefeller 104A
Rutgers............107D
St Catherine 131C
St Gabriel's 123C

St Nicholas 148B
Sakura 144A
SD Roosevelt ..107A
Sheltering Arms ......
........................148D
Seward 107B
Stuyvesant Sq...119C
Thomas Jefferson....
........................147C
Thomas Paine...105A
Tompkins Sq 114B
Tribeca............104C
Triboro Bridge 147A
Trinity Cemetery
........................152B
Tudor 123A
Union Sq 118B
James J Walker ......
........................108B
Vladeck 111D
Washington Sq ......
........................113C
24th St 119A

THINGS TO DO
Birding
The Ramble,
Central Pk, ...133C

Butterflying
Inwood Hill Park,
........................160D

ZOOS
**Central Park Zoo
Wildlife
Conservation
Center**
830 Fifth Av,,
212-439-6500   129D

**ARENAS &
STADIUMS**
Madison Sq Garden
7 Av @ W 32 St,
212-465-6741   121
NY Cityhawks (Apr-Jul)
NY Liberty (Jun-Aug)
NY Knicks (Nov-Apr)
NY Rangers (Oct-Apr)
WTA Tennis (Nov)

CITY LINKS
Bucket of Balls
Chelsea Piers
12 Av @ 23 St,
212-336-6400   116

Family Golf Center
Randall's Island,
212-427-5689   302

EXTREME
Parasailing
Parasail NYC
Pier 25, Joe
DiMaggio Hwy @
N. Noore St,
212-691-0055   106

**FIELD OF
DREAMS**
Batting Practice
Chelsea Piers
12 Av @ 23 St,
212-336-6500   116

**Hackers, Hitters
& Hoops**
123 W 18 St,
212-929-7482   117

**Randall's Island
Practice Center**
212-427-5689   302

Cricket
Randall's Island
302

GOTHAM GRID IRON
Football Pick Up

Central Park 133A

Rugby
Randall's Island
302B

GYM FOR A DAY
Asphalt Green
555 E 90 St,
212-369-8890 139D

Club La Raquette
119 W 56 St,
212-245-1144 125B

Crunch Fitness
54 E 13 St,
212-475-2018 113B

NY Health & Racquet
120 E 50 St,
212-593-1500 126B
39 Whitehall St,
212-269-9800 103C
(locations in MA)

NY Sports Club
1635 Third Av,
212-987-7200 139D

Printing House
Fitness & Racquet
421 Hudson St,
212-243-7600 108B

Sports Center at
Chelsea Piers
62 Av @ 23 St,
212-336-6000 116C

World Gym
232 Mercer St,
212-780-7407 113D

YM & YWCA
1610 Lex. Av, 212-
755-4500 126B

HOOP DREAMS
*There are a number of courts in NYC where great **street basketball** can be experienced indoors and out. Here's a sampling of the best:*

Outdoors
"The Cage"
W 4 St, 113C

Fort Tryon Park
Margaret Corbin Plz
158D

Holcombe
Rucker Park
155 St @ Eighth Av,
153A

MARATHON MADNESS
NY Road Runners
Club Fred Lebow Pl,
9 E 89 St,
212-860-4455 137D

The NY Marathon is 30,000 runners coursing through five boroughs on the first weekend in November. Starts on the Verrazano Bridge and ends in Central Park
129A

RACQUETS
Tennis
NY Health &
Racquet Tennis
Wall St @ Piers 13
& 14,
212-422-9300 103B

City Courts
Central Park
96 St & West Dr,
212-280-0205 137A

GLOBAL GOALS
Soccer Pick-Ups
East River Park,
Sunday 11am 111D

SKATING – ICE
Lasker Rink
110 St & Lenox Av, ,
212-534-7639
141B

Rockefeller Center
212-332-7654
125B

Sky Rink
Chelsea Piers,
212-336-6100 116C

Wollman Rink
S Central Park,
212-396-1010 129D

STREET WHEELS
Bikes
119 miles of bike routes exist. today with plans for 781 more miles:

Central Park
129A

Blades
Empire Skate Club
of NY (ESCNY)
212-592-3674

NY Skate Patrol
212-439-1234

Central Park 129B

Battery Park
Esplanade 104C

Brooklyn Bridge
105A

Boards
Brooklyn Bridge
@ Park Row,
105A

Central Park
The Mall, 129B

URBAN HOOVES
Stables
Claremont
Riding Academy
175 W 89 St,
212-724-5100 136D

VOLLEYBALL
Big City
Volleyball League
212-288-4240

NY Urban
Professional
Athletic League
212-877-3614

Central Park
on 68 St, 129B

Dalton Gym
E 87 St @ Third Av
139C

HS Environmental
Studies
444 W 56 St,
124B

WATER SPORTS
Canoe & Kayak
Metropolitan
Canoe & Kayak Club
212-724-5069

NY Kayak Co
601 W 26 St,
116A

Sail

Manhattan
Sailing School
North Cove,
212-786-0400
104C

Great Hudson
Sailing Center
Chelsea Piers,
212-741-7245
116A

Swim
Indoors–

Chelsea Piers
12 Av @ 23 St,
212-336-6400
116C

63 St YMCA
5 W 63 St,
212-787-1301
129C

Asphalt Green
555 E 90 St,
212-369-8890
139D

Vanderbilt YMCA
224 E 47 St,
212-756-9600
127C

Outdoors–

Hamilton Fish Pool
128 Pitt St,
212-387-7687 111A

TO FIND A TOP 100

simply turn to page
and locate a park or
garden in grids
A,B,C or D.

RECREATION

NIGHTLIFE

BLUES, FOLK, ROCK & SOUL

Venues may offer many styles of music. Call for more details.

Arlene Grocery
95 Stanton St,
212-358-1633   **110B**

Arthur's Tavern
57 Grove St,
212-675-6879   **112D**

Bitter End
147 Bleecker St,
212-673-7030   **113D**

The Blue Lounge
625 Broadway,
212-473-8787   **113D**

Bottom Line
15 W 4 St,
212-228-7880   **113D**

Brownies
169 Av A,
212-420-8392   **114B**

CBGB
315 Bowery,
212-982-4052   **114C**

Cheetah
12 W 21 St,
212-206-7770   **117B**

Chicago B.L.U.E.S.
73 Eighth Av,
212-924-9755   **112B**

Coney Island High
15 St Mark's Pl,
212-674-7959   **114A**

The Cooler
416 W 14 St,
212-645-5189   **112B**

Fez
380 Lafayette St,
212-533-2680   **114C**

Gonzalez y Gonzalez
625 Broadway,
212-473-8787   **113D**

Irving Plaza
17 Irving Pl,
212-777-6800   **119D**

Knitting Factory
74 Leonard St,
212-219-3055   **106D**

Le Bar Bat
311 W 57 St,
212-307-7228   **129C**

Louisiana Grill
622 Broadway,
212-460-9633   **113D**

Manny's Car Wash
1558 Third Av,
212-369-BLUES,   **139C**

Mercury Lounge
217 E Houston St, ,
212-260-4700
                        114D

Rock'n Roll Cafe
149 Bleecker St,
212-677-7630   **113C**

Terra Blues
149 Bleecker St,
212-777-7776   **113C**

West End Gate
2911 Broadway,
212-662-8830   **144D**

Wetlands Preserve
161 Hudson St,
212-966-4225   **106A**

CABARET

Bemelmans Bar
35 E 76 St,
212-744-1600   **134D**

Café Carlyle
35 E 76 St,
212-570-7189   **134D**

Chez Josephine
414 W 42 St,
212-594-1925   **120B**

The Chestnut Room
Tavern on the Green
CPW @ 67 St,
212-873-3200   **129A**

Danny's Skylight Room
346 W 46 St,
212-265-8133   **125C**

Don't Tell Mama
343 W 46 St,
212-757-0788   **125C**

Eighty Eight's
228 W 10 St,
212-924-0088   **112D**

Judy's Chelsea
169 Eighth Av,
212-929-5410   **117C**

Mother
432 W 14 St,
212-366-5680   **112A**

The Oak Room
59 W 44 St,
212-840-6800   **125D**

Rainbow & Stars
30 Rockefeller
Center Plz,
212-632-5000   **125D**

Triad
58 W 72 St,
212-799-4599   **128B**

COMEDY CLUBS

Boston Comedy
82 W 3 St,
212-477-1000   **113C**

Caroline's
1626 Broadway,
212-757-4100   **125A**

Catch a Rising Star
253 W 28 St,
212-244-3005   **117A**

Comedy Cellar
117 MacDougal St,
212-254-3480   **113C**

Chicago City Limits
1105 First Av,
212-888-5233   **131C**

Dangerfield's
1118 First Av,
212-593-1650   **131C**

Gotham
34 W 22 St,
212-367-9000   **117B**

New York Comedy Club
241 E 24 St,
212-696-LAFF   **118B**

The Original Improv
433 W 34 St,
212-279-3446   **120D**

Rebar
127 Eighth Av,
212-627-1680   **117C**

Soho Arts Group
36 W 17 St,
212-463-8732   **117D**

Stand-Up NY
236 W 78 St,
212-595-0850   **132D**

DANCE CLUBS

The Apollo
253 W 125 St,
212-749-5838,   **149**

Au Bar
41 E 58 St,
212-308-9455   **130**

Baby Jupiter
170 Orchard St, ,
212-780-0287   **110**

The Bank
225 E Houston St,
212-505-5033   **114**

Copacabana
617 W 57,
212-582-2672   **124**

The Latin Quarter
2551 Broadway,
212-864-7600   **136**

Life
158 Bleecker St,
212-420-1999   **113**

Nell's
246 W 14 St,
212-675-1567   **112**

Pyramid Club
101 Av A,
212-473-7184   **114**

Roseland
239 W 52 St,
212-247-0200   **125**

The Roxy
515 W 18 St,
212-645-5156   **116**

S.O.B.'s
(Sounds of Brazil)
204 Varick St,
212-243-4940   **109**

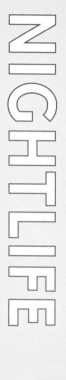
NIGHTLIFE

unnel
20 Twelfth Av,
12-695-4682 **116A**

vilo
30 W 27 Av,
2268-1600 **116B**

inyl
7 Hudson St,
2-343-1379 **114A**

ebster Hall
25 E 11 St,
2-353-1600 **114A**

**AZZ &
TANDARDS**

lgonquin
9 W 44 St,
2-840-6800 **125D**

t.Coffee
39 Av A,
2-529-2233 **114B**

he Baggot Inn
2 W 3 St,
2-477-0622 **113C**

ell Cafe
0 Spring St,
2-334-2355 **109C**

emelman's Bar
5 E 76 St,
2-744-1600 **134D**

irdland
5 W 44 St,
2-581-3080 **125C**

he Blue Note
31 W 3 St,
2-475-8592 **113C**

owery Bar
0 E 4 St,
2-475-2220 **114C**

Bull and Bear
Lex. Av @ 49 St,
212-872-4900 **126D**

Café Carlyle
35 E 76 St,
212-744-1600 **134C**

Club El Flamingo
547 W 21 St,
212-307-7171 **116D**

Detour
349 E 13 St,
212-533-6212 **114B**

Feinstein's
540 Park Av,
212-759-4100 **130D**

Homefront
236 W 54 St,
212-560-2271 **125A**

Iridium
44 W 63 St,
212-582-2121 **128D**

Izzy Bar
166 First Av,
212-228-0444 **114B**

Internet Cafe
82 E 3 St,
212-614-0747 **114C**

The Jazz Standard
116 E 27 St,
212-576-2232 **118B**

Jules
65 St Marks Pl,
212-477-5560 **114A**

Knitting Factory
74 Leonard St,
212-219-3055 **106D**

Lenox Lounge
288 Lenox Av,
212-722-9566 **145B**

Michaels Pub
57 E 54 St,
212-758-2272 **126B**

Metronome
915 Broadway,
212-505-7400 **118C**

Opaline
85 Av A,
212-475-5050 **114D**

St Nick's Pub
773 St Nicholas Av,
212-283-9728 **152D**

Savoy Lounge
355 W 41 St,
212-947-5255 **120B**

Smalls
183 W 10 St,
212-929-7565 **113A**

Sugar Shack
2611 Eighth Av,
212-491-4422 **149A**

Sweet Basil
88 Seventh Av S,
212-242-1785 **113C**

Village Vanguard
178 Seventh Av S,
212-255-4037 **112B**

Visiones
125 MacDougal St,
800-831-BEBOP **113C**

Wells
2247 Seventh Av,
212-234-0700 **149A**

Zinc Bar
90 W Houston,
212-477-8337 **109A**

Zinno
126 W 13 St,
212-924-5182 **113A**

LATE NIGHT EATS

Around the Clock
8 Stuyvesant St,
212-598-0402 **114C**

Blue Ribbon
97 Sullivan St,
212-274-0404 **109A**

Carnegie Deli
854 Seventh Av,
212-757-2245 **125A**

Coffee Shop
26 Union Sq W,
212-243-7969 **118C**

Erizo Latino
422 W Broadway,
212-941-5811 **109A**

Florent
69 Gansevoort St,
212-989-5779 **112A**

NY Noodle Town
28 1/2 Bowery,
212-349-0923 **107C**

The Odeon
145 W Broadway.
212-233-0507 **106D**

Pravda
281 Lafayette St,
212-226-4696 **109B**

Raoul's
180 Prince St,
212-966-3518 **109A**

Wollensky's Grill
205 E 49 St,
212-753-0444 **127C**

PUBS & BARS

Campbell Apartment
17 Vanderbilt Av,
212-980-9476 **122B**

Double Happiness
173 Mott St,
212-941-1282 **107A**

Ear Inn
326 Spring St,
212-226-9060 **108D**

**Greatest Bar
on Earth**
1 WTC 107th fl,
212-524-7011 **104A**

Joe's Pub
425 Lafayette St,
212-239-6200 **114C**

Lansky Lounge
138 Delancey St,
212-677-9489 **110B**

Standard
158 First Av,
212-387-0239 **114B**

McSorley's
15 E 7 St,
212-473-9148 **114C**

White Horse Tavern
567 Hudson St,
212-243-9260 **112B**

SUPPER CLUBS

Laura Belle
120 W 43 St,
212-819-1000 **126C**

The Rainbow Grill
30 Rock Plz, 65 fl,
212-632-5000 **126A**

Supper Club
240 W 47 St,
212-921-1940 **125C**

151
151 E 50 St,
212-753-1144 **126B**

TO FIND A TOP 100

simply turn to page
and locate a club or
pub in grids
A,B,C or D.

PERFORMING

Aaron Davis Hall
CUNY, W 135 St @
Convent Av,
212-650-7100 **148**B

Alice Tully Hall
Lincoln Center,
212-875-5000 **128**B
Chamber Music Society

**American Opera
Projects**
463 Broome St,
212-431-8102 **109**D

Amato Opera
319 Bowery,
212-228-8200 **110**A

Avery Fisher Hall
Lincoln Center,
(212) 875-5030 **128**B
NYC Philharmonic

Beacon Theater
Broadway @ 74 St,
212-307-7171 **132**D

Brecht Forum
122 W 27 St,
212-242-4201 **117**B

CSC Repertory
136 E 13 St,
212-677-4210 **114**A

CAMI Hall
165 W 57 St,
212-841-9650 **129**C

Carnegie Hall
881 Seventh Av
@ W 57 St,
212-903-9600 **125**A

Chelsea Piers
Joe Di Maggio Hwy
@ W 23 St,
212-336-6666 **116**C

**Church of St.
Matthew/St.Timothy**
26 W 84 St, **132**B

**The Church of St.
Ignatius Loyola**
980 Park Av, **134**B

**Circle in the
Square**
1633 Broadway,
212-307-2700 **125**A

City Center
131 W 55 St,
212-581-1212 **125**B

Context Studios
28 Avenue A,
212-953-0651 **114**D

Continental Center
180 Maiden Lane,
212-799-5000 **103**B

**Danspace at St
Mark's Church-in-
the-Bowery**
131 E 10 St,
212-674-8194 **114**A

**Dance Theater
Workshop (DTW)**
219 W 19 St,
212-924-0077 **117**C

**Delacorte Theater
Shakespeare in
the Park**
Central Park,
212-861-PAPP **133**A

Deutsches House
42 Washington Mews,
212-998-8660 **113**B

Dia Ctr for the Arts
548 W 22 St,
212-989-5912 **116**B

Ensemble Studio
549 W 52 St,
212-247-4982 **124**B

FIT, Haft Auditorium
227 W 27 @ 7 Av,
212-307-2700 **117**A

Flea Theatre
41 White St,
212-226-0051 **106**D

Florence Gould Hall
Alliance Française
55 E 59 St,
212-355-6160 **130**D

Goethe Haus
1014 Fifth Av,
212-439-8700 **133**D

**Hammerstein
Ballroom**
311 W 34 St,
212-279-7740 **121**C

**Henry Street
Settlement**
Louis Abrams
Arts Center,
466 Grand St,
212-598-0400 **111**C

HERE
145 Sixth Av,
212-647-0202 **109**A

Irish Arts Center
553 W 51 St,
212-757-3318 **124**B

**The Joseph Papp
Public Theater**
425 Lafayette St,
212-260-2400 **113**B

Joyce Theater
175 Eighth Av,
212-242-0800 **117**C

Joyce SoHo
155 Mercer St,
212-431-9233 **109**B

Juilliard Theatre
Lincoln Center,
155 W 65 St,
212-769-7406 **128**B

Jupiter Symphony
152 W 66 St,
212-799-1259 **12**B

Kaplan Penthouse
Lincoln Center,
212-875-5288 **128**B

The Kitchen
512 W 19 St,
212-255-5793 **116**D

La MaMa E.T.C.
74 1/2 E 4 St,
212- 475-7710 **114**C

**LaPlaza Cultural
Community Garden**
Avenue C @ 9 St,
212-501-2429 **115**A

**Lincoln Center for
the Performing Arts**
Lincoln Center,
212-875-5400 **128**B

**Manhattan School
of Music–Borden
Auditorium**
120 Claremont Av,
212-749-2802 **144**A

**New School Mannes
Performance Space**
150 W 85 St,
212-580-0210 **126**D

**The Metropolitan
Museum of Art**
1000 Fifth Av,
212-535-7710 **133**B

**The Metropolitan
Opera House**
Lincoln Center,
212-362-6000 **128**B
American Ballet Theatre
& Metropolitan Opera

**Miller Theater–
Columbia Univ**
B'way @ 116 St,
212-854-1754 **144**A

Mitzi Newhouse
Lincoln Center,
150 W 65,
212-362-7600 **128**B

**New Victory
Theater**
209 W 42 St,
212-564-4222 **125**B

**New-York
Historical Society**
170 CPW,
212-873-3400 **133**B

**The New York
Public Library for
the Performing Arts**
B'way @ 65 St,
212-870-1630 **128**B

**NY Society for
Ethical Culture**
2 W 64 St,
212-874-5210 **129**B

NY State Theater
Lincoln Center,
212-870-5570
NYC Ballet • NYC Opera
128B

**Nuyorican
Poets Cafe**
236 E 3 St,
212-505-8183 **114**B

ARTS & FILM

ce Downtown
ater
pruce St,
-346-1715 **105**C

Asian
pertory Theater
W 46 St,
-505-5655 **124**D

foming Garage
Wooster St,
-966-3651 **109**D

122
First Av,
-477-5288 **114**B

erside Church
Riverside Dr,
-222-5900 **145**A

io City
sic Hall
h Av @ 50 St,
-247-4777 **125**B

ortorio Español
E 27 St,
-889-2850 **118**B

rancis of Assisi
W 31 St, **122**C

Mark's Church–
he–Bowery
ond Av @ 10 St,
-674-8194 **114**B

atrick's
nedral
Av @ E 50 St, ,
-753-2261 **125**B

aul's Chapel
ay @ Fulton St, ,
-602-0872 **104**C

eter's Church
W 20 St,
-691-6263 **117**C

St Thomas Church
Fifth Av @ 53 St,
212-664-9360
  125B

**Shakespeare
in the Park–
Delacorte Theater**
Central Park,
212-861-PAPP
  133A

**The Spanish
Institute**
684 Park Av,
(212) 628-0420 **130**B

**The Studio Museum
in Harlem**
144 W 125 St,
(212) 864-4500 **145**A

**Kaye Playhouse–
Hunter College**
Park Av @ 68 St,
212-772-4448
  130B

Symphony Space
2537 Broadway,
212-864-5400 **136**B

TADA!
120 W 28 St,
212-627-1732 **117**B

**Theatre for the
New City**
155 First Av,
212-254-1109 **114**B

Town Hall
123 W 43 St,
212-840-2824 **125**C

**Tribeca Performing
Arts Center**
199 Chambers St,
212-346-8510 **104**A

Trinity Church
89 B'way @ Wall St,
212-602-0872
  102A

**Vivian Beaumont
Theater**
Lincoln Center
150 W 65 St,
212-362-7600 **128**B

**Walter Reade
Theater**
Lincoln Center,
212-875-5600 **128**B

Weill Recital Hall
881 Seventh Av
@ W 57 St,
212-247-7800 **112**D

Westbeth Theatre
151 Bank St,
212-741-0391 **112**D

Winter Garden
1634 Broadway,
212-239-6200 **125**A

**Winter Garden at
the WFC**
212-945-0505 **104**C

**92nd St Y &
YWCA**
1395 Lex. Av,
212-996-1100 **139**A

FILM

Alice Tully Hall
Lincoln Center,
212-875-5000 **128**B
NY Film Festival, Human
Rights Watch Festival

**American Museum
of Natural History**
CPW @ 79 St,
212-769-5650 **133**C

Angelika Film Center
18 W Houston St,
212-995-2000 **113**D

**Anthology Film
Archives**
32 Second Av,
212-505-5110 **114**C

Bryant Park
Sixth Av @ 42 St,
212-983-41420 **121**B

Film Forum
209 W Houston St,
212-727-8110 **109**A

French Institute
55 E 59 St,
212-355-6160 **130**D

**Goethe House
Institute**
1014 Fifth Av,
212-439-8700 **133**B

**Museum of Modern
Art (MoMA)**
11 W 53 St,
212-708-9400 **125**B

**The New York
Film Academy**
100 E 17 St,
212-674-4300 **118**D

**NYU Cantor
Film Center**
36 E 8 St,
212-998-8872 **113**B

**New York
Public Library–
Donnell Library**
20 W 53 St,
212-621-0618 **126**A

Screening Room
54 Varick St,
212-334-2100 **106**A

Sony IMAX
1998 Broadway
(68 St),
212-336-5000 **128**B

Thalia Theater
250 W 95 St,
212-864-7700 **136**B

Walter Reade Theatre
Lincoln Center,
212-875-5600 **128**B

YMCA Cine-Club
610 Lexington. Av,
212-755-4500 **126**B

The Ziegfeld
141 W 54 St,
212-765-7600 **125**B

NOTES:
_____

TO FIND A TOP 100

simply turn to page
and locate a cinema
or theater in grids
A,B,C or D.

SHOPPING

ART & PAPER

Alphabets
115 Av A,
212-475-7250 **114**B

Kate's Paperie
561 Broadway,
212-941-9816 **109**B
3 locations

NY Central Art Supply
62 Third Av,
212-473-7705 **114**C

Pearl Paint
308 Canal St,
212-431-7932 **106**B

Poster America
138 W 18 St,
212-206-0499 **117**D

BOOKS & MUSIC

Argosy
116 E 59 St,
212-753-4455 **130**D

Barnes & Noble
33 E 17 St,
212-253-0810 **118**D
plus 9 locs citywide.

Sale Annex
128 Fifth Av,
212-253-0810 **118**C

Borders WTC
5 WTC,
212-839-8037 **104**D

Coliseum
1771 Broadway,
212-757-8381 **129**C

Colony Records
1619 Broadway,
212-265-2050 **125**C

Empire State News
Empire State Bldg,
212-279-9153 **121**D

HMV
2081 Broadway,
212-721-5900 **128**B
Herald Sq Store

Hudson News
Penn Station,
212-971-6800 **121**C

Rizzoli International
454 W B'way,
212-674-1616 **109**B

St Mark's Book Shop
31 Third Av,
212-260-7853 **114**A

Shakespeare & Co.
716 Broadway,
212-529-1330 **113**D

The Strand
828 Broadway,
212-473-1452 **113**A

**Subterranean
Records**
5 Cornelia St,
212-463-8900 **113**B

Tower Records
692 Broadway,
212-505-1500 **113**D

Universal News
977 Eighth Av
212-459-0932 **129**C

Virgin Megastore
1540 Broadway,
212-921-1020 **125**C

DESIGNERS

Agnès B.
116-18 Prince St,
212-925-4649 **109**B

Anna Sui
113 Greene St,
212-941-8406 **109**B

Armani
760 Madison Av,
212-988-9191 **130**B

Betsey Johnson
138 Wooster St,
212-995-5048 **109**B

Calvin Klein
654 Madison Av,
212-292-9000 **130**D

Comme des Garçons
520 W 22 St,
212-604-9200 **116**B

Donna Karan
655 Madison Av,
212-223-3569 **130**D

Helmut Lang
80 Greene St,
212-925-7214 **109**B

Paul Smith
108 Fifth Av,
212-627-9770 **117**D

Ralph Lauren
867 Madison Av
@ 72 St,
212-606-2100 **130**B

Tocca
161 Mercer,
212-343-3912 **109**D

Slaughterhouse
448 W 16 St,
212-376-4985 **116**D

Yohji Yamamoto
103 Grand St,
800-803-4443 **106**B

DEPARTMENT STORES

Barneys NY
660 Madison Av,
212-826-8900 **130**A

Bergdorf Goodman
754 Fifth Av,
212-753-7300 **130**C

Bloomingdale's
1000 Third Av,
212-705-2000 **130**D

Brooks Brothers
346 Madison Av,
212-682-8800 **126**D

Canal Jean
504 Broadway,
212-226-1130 **109**D

Century 21
22 Cortlandt St,
212-227-9092 **104**D

Felissimo
10 W 56 St,
212-247-5656 **126**A

Jeffrey NY
449 W 14 St,
212-206-1272 **116**D

Lord & Taylor
424 Fifth Av,
212-391-3344 **122**A

Macy's–Herald Sq
151 W 34 St,
212-695-4400 **121**C

Pearl River
277 Canal St,
212-219-8107 **106**B

Saks Fifth Avenue
Fifth Av @ 49 St,
212-753-4000 **125**D

Syms
42 Trinity Pl,
212-797-1199 **1**

Takashimaya
693 Fifth Av,
212-350-0100 **12**

Terra Verde
122 Wooster St,
212-925-4533 **1**

F.A.O. Schwarz
767 Fifth Av,
212-644-9400 **12**

ELECTRONICS

Harvey's
888 Broadway,
212-228-5354 **1**

J&R Music World
23 Park Row,
212-238-9000 **1**

Stereo Exchange
627 Broadway,
212-505-1111 **1**

GIFTS & TOYS

Enchanted Forest
85 Mercer St,
212-925-6677 **1**

Forbidden Planet
B'way @ 13 St,
212-473-1576 **1**

Little Rickie
49 1/2 First Av,
212-505-6467 **1**

GOURMET

**Astor Wines &
Liquors**
12 Astor Pl,
212-674-7500 **1**

SHOPPING

ducci's
Sixth Av,
-673-2600 **113A**

ney Greengrass
Amsterdam Av,
-724-4707 **136D**

ley Bakery
W Broadway,
-964-2525 **106D**

rella
5 Broadway,
-874-0383 **132D**

n & DeLuca
Broadway,
-431-1691 **109B**

way Market
7 Broadway,
-595-1888 **132D**

way Market
town)
3 Twelfth Av,
-234-3883 **148C**

en Markets
-477-3220
ion Sq, **118C**
effield Plaza,
124B

rmet Garage
Broome St,
-941-5850 **109C**

s Pickle Products
ssex St,
254-4477 **110D**

rell & Co
ckefeller Pl,
-688-9370 **126C**

sserie Lanciani
W 14 St,
-989-1213 **112B**

Sherry–Lehmann
679 Madison Av,
212-838-7500 **130D**

Yonah Schimmel
137 E Houston St,
212-477-2858 **110A**

Zabar's
2245 Broadway,
212-787-2000 **132B**

HOME & DESIGN

ABC-Home & Carpet
888 Broadway,
212-473-3000 **118C**

Ad Hoc Softwares
410 W B'way,
212-925-2652 **106B**

Bed Bath & Beyond
Sixth Av @ 18 St,
212-255-3550 **117D**

Crate & Barrel
650 Madison Av,
212-308-0011 **130D**

Chelsea Antiques
Market
110 W 25 St,
212-929-0909 **117B**

Depression Modern
150 Sullivan St,
212-982-5699 **109A**

Henri Bendel
712 Fifth Av,
212-247-1100 **126A**

Moss
146 Greene St,
212-226-2190 **109B**

Prince Lumber
15 St @ Ninth Av,
212-777-1150 **116D**

Shabby Chic
93 Greene St,
212-274-9842 **109B**

Simon's Hardware
421 Third Av,
212-532-9220 **122D**

Smith & Hawken
394 W B'way,
212-925-0687 **109C**

The Terence
Conran Shop
415 E 57 St,
212-755-9079 **131D**

Urban Archaeology
285 Lafayette St,
212-431-6969 **109B**

**INSTRUMENTS–
MUSICAL**

Sam Ash
160 W 48 St,
212-719-2299 **125C**

Manny's
156 W 48 St,
212-819-0576 **125C**

The Music Store
44 W 62 St,
212-541-6236 **128D**

JEWELRY

Bulgari
730 Fifth Av,
212-315-9000 **126A**

Cartier
725 Fifth Av,
212-308-0843 **126B**

Harry Winston
718 Fifth Av,
212-245-2000 **126A**

Tiffany & Co.
727 Fifth Av,
212-755-8000 **126A**

Tourneau
12 E 57 St,
212-758-7300 **130D**

Van Cleef & Arpels
744 Fifth Av,
212-644-9500 **126C**

**PERSONAL
CARE & VANITY**

Astor Place Hair
Designers
2 Astor Pl,
212-475-9854 **113B**

Bliss
568 Broadway
212-219-8970 **109B**

Gauntlet
144 Fifth Av,
212-229-0180 **117D**

Georgette Klinger
501 Madison Av,
212-838-3200 **126B**

Jason Croy
632 Hudson St,
212-691-8299 **112B**

Kiehl's
109 Third Av,
212-677-3171 **114A**

Elizabeth Arden
691 Fifth Av,
212-546-0200 **126A**

Origins Feel-Good Spa
Pier 60, Chelsea Piers
212-336-6780 **116C**

Russian Baths
268 E 10 St,
212-505-0665 **114B**

Vidal Sassoon
767 Fifth Av,
212-535-9200 **129D**

SPORTS

Blades– 6 locations
120 W 72 St,
212-787-3911 **128B**

NikeTown, NY
6 E 57 St,
212-891-6453 **130D**

Paragon
867 Broadway,
212-255-8036 **118C**

TECHNO GEAR

Airmarket
97 Third Av,
212-995-5888 **114A**

House
84 E 7 St,
212-677-7379 **114C**

Nylonsquid
222 Lafayette St,
212-334-6554 **109D**

URBAN WEAR

Transit
665 Broadway,
212-358-8726 **113D**

THEME STORES

The Disney Store
711 Fifth Av,
212-702-0702 **125C**

Hard Rock Cafe
221 W 57 St,
212-459-9320 **125A**

Warner Bros. Store
1 E 57 St,
800-223-6524 **129D**

TO FIND A TOP 100

simply turn to page
and locate the
theatre in grids
A,B,C or D.

THEATRE

ON BROADWAY

Ambassador
215 W 49 St,
212-239-6200 **125C**

Belasco
111 W 44 St,
212-239-6200 **125D**

Booth
222 W 45 St,
212-239-6200 **125C**

Broadhurst
235 W 44 St,
212-239-6200 **125C**

Broadway
1681 Broadway,
212-239-6200 **125A**

Brooks Atkinson
256 W 47 St,
212-307-4100 **125C**

Circle in the Square
1633 Broadway,
212-239-6200 **125A**

Cort
138 W 48 St,
212-239-6200 **125C**

Criterion Center
1530 Broadway,
212-764-7903 **125C**

Ethel Barrymore
243 W 47 St,
212-239-6200 **125C**

Eugene O'Neill
230 W 49 St,
212-239-6200 **125C**

Gershwin
222 W 51 St,
212-586-6510 **125A**

Golden
252 W 45 St,
212-239-6200 **125C**

Helen Hayes
240 W 44 St,
212-307-4100 **125C**

Imperial
249 W 45 St,
212-239-6200 **125C**

Longacre
220 W 48 St,
212-239-6200 **125C**

Lunt-Fontanne
205 W 46 St,
212-575-9200 **125C**

Lyceum
149 W 45 St,
212-239-6200 **125C**

Majestic
247 W 44 St,
212-239-6200 **125C**

Marquis
1535 Broadway,
212-382-0100 **125C**

Martin Beck
302 W 45 St,
212-239-6200 **125C**

Minskoff
200 W 45 St,
212-869-0550 **125C**

Music Box
239 W 45 St,
212-239-6200 **125C**

Nederlander
208 W 41 St,
212-307-4100 **121A**

Neil Simon
250 W 52 St,
212-757-8646 **125A**

New Amsterdam
214 W 42 St,
212-307-4100 **125C**

New Victory
209 W 42 St,
212-564-4222 **125C**

Palace
1564 Broadway,
212-730-8200 **125C**

Plymouth
236 W 45 St,
212-239-6200 **125C**

Richard Rodgers
226 W 46 St,
212-307-4100 **125C**

Roundabout
1530 Broadway,
212-869-8400 **125C**

Royale
242 W 45 St,
212-239-6200 **125C**

St James
246 W 44 St,
212-239-6200 **125C**

Shubert
225 W 44 St,
212-239-6200 **125C**

Virginia
245 W 52 St,
212-239-6200 **125A**

Vivian Beaumont
Lincoln Center,
212-239-6200 **128B**

Walter Kerr
219 W 48 St,
212-239-6200 **125C**

Winter Garden
1634 Broadway,
212-239-6200 **125A**

OFF & OFF-OFF

American Jewish
307 W 26 St,
212-633-9797 **117A**

American Place
111 W 46 St,
212-840-2960 **125D**

Actors Playhouse
100 Seventh Av,
212-239-6200 **117C**

Astor Place
434 Lafayette St,
212-254-4370 **113B**

Atlantic
336 W 20 St,
212-239-6200 **117C**

Beacon
2124 Broadway,
212-307-7171 **132D**

Bouwerie Lane
330 Bowery,
212-677-0060 **1**

Castillo Cultural Center
500 Greenwich S
212-941-1234 **1**

Century
111 E 15 St,
212-239-6200 **1**

Cherry Lane
38 Commerce St,
212-239-6200 **1**

City Center Stage
131 W 55 St,
212-581-1212 **1**

Classic Stage Co
136 E 13 St,
212-677-4210 **1**

Currican
154 W 29 St,
212-736-2533 **1**

Daryl Roth
101 E 15 St,
212-375-1110 **1**

Douglas Fairban
432 W 42 St,
212-239-4321 **1**

Duffy
1553 Broadway,
212-695-3401 **1**